The Poetry Break

The Poetry Break

*An Annotated Anthology
with Ideas for Introducing
Children to Poetry*

by CAROLINE FELLER BAUER

Illustrations by EDITH BINGHAM

H. W. Wilson
1995

For Peter,
My Poetry Pal

Library of Congress Cataloging-in-Publication Data

Bauer, Caroline Feller.
      The poetry break : an annotated anthology with ideas for introducing children to poetry / by Caroline Feller Bauer.
          p.   cm.
      Includes bibliographical references and index.
      ISBN 0-8242-0852-8
      1. Children's poetry—Study and teaching.   2. Oral interpretation of poetry.
I. Title.
PN1085.B38   1995
372.64—dc20
                                                                                            93-42069
                                                                                            CIP

Printed in the United States of America
First Printing

The Gentleman Bookworm

by J. Patrick Lewis

There once was a Gentleman Bookworm
Ate his words with a fork and a spoon.
    When friends crawled down
    From Book End Town
He offered them *Goodnight Moon*.

He fed them *The Wind in the Willows*
And a page out of *Charlotte's Web*.
    They were eating bizarre
    Where the Wild Things Are
When one of the guestworms said,

"How sinfully rich and delicious!
Why should anyone bother to cook?
    You've done it, dear boy!
    Now sit down and enjoy
A bite of this poetry book!"

Contents

Contents

Contents

Part Two   Using The Poems

Preface

I told my husband Peter that I was going to call this book *The Poetry Break: An Annotated Anthology*. He said, "Before I married you I wouldn't have known what that subtitle meant."

Since you have not been married to me for thirty years, I thought I'd better explain. This book is meant to make it easier for parents, teachers, and librarians to introduce poetry to children in such a pleasurable way that reading and enjoying poetry will become a lifelong habit. The idea is a simple one: Take less than a half minute to read aloud or recite poetry on a daily basis.

I've demonstrated this easy-to-execute idea in workshops and have received many letters and newspaper articles describing the success of the idea in homes, schools, public libraries and even offices.

Janet Knobel at the International School in Seoul, Korea just called to tell me that eighty-five students, grades K–12, participated in the poetry break this spring. Karen Vlieg in Calgary, Canada reports that, "Many kids at the school are now doing poetry breaks with my top hat and white gloves—and having a ball." Marvia Boettcher in Bismarck, North Dakota passed along the idea of the poetry break to her college class and wrote to me, "Poetry break is a must during each class and, once again, you can chalk up a success story." One of Marvia's students told her, "I love the idea of poetry break! All week my daughter and I have been shouting at each other 'Poetry Break' and then racing to see who can recite something first!"

Many people who use the poetry break report that the poetry section in the library has doubled and tripled its circulation and that they have purchased more poetry books to satisfy the demand. Since so many are already trying the poetry break with good success, I thought it would be useful to have one book available that would make it easier to choose poems and suggest presentation ideas.

So, Peter, this is an annotated anthology: a collection of poems with notes to help you present poetry at the office.

Acknowledgments

Grateful acknowledgment is made to the following for permission to reprint copyrighted material listed below.

Every effort has been made to trace the ownership of all copyrighted material and to secure the necessary permissions to reprint these selections.

"About the Teeth of Sharks" by John Ciardi, reprinted courtesy of the Ciardi Family.

"Abracadabra" from *A Fine Fat Pig and Other Animal Poems* by Mary Ann Hoberman. Text copyright © 1991 by Mary Ann Hoberman. Selection reprinted by permission of HarperCollins Publishers.

"Advice from Aunt Prudence" by Bobbi Katz © 1993. Used by permission of Bobby Katz who controls all rights.

"Aerobics" from *A Mouse in My Roof* by Richard Edwards. Copyright © 1988 by Richard Edwards. Used by permission of Delacorte Press, a division of Bantam Doubleday Dell Publishing Group, Inc.

"Alarm Clock" from *A Sky Full Of Poems* by Eve Merriam. Copyright © 1964, 1970, 1973 by Eve Merriam. Reprinted by permission of Marian Reiner.

"All Star Boys" from *Cocoanut Kind of Day* by Lynn Joseph. Copyright © 1990 by Lynn Joseph. Reprinted by permission of Lothrop, Lee & Shepard Books, a division of William Morrow & Company, Inc.

"Alligator on the Escalator" from *JAMBOREE: Rhymes for All Times* by Eve Merriam. Copyright © 1962, 1964, 1966, 1973, 1984 by Eve Merriam. Reprinted by permission of Marian Reiner.

"The Alphabet Monster" by Robert Heidbreder from *Don't Eat Spiders*, poems copyright © Robert Heidbreder 1985. Reprinted by permission of Oxford University Press Canada.

"Amanda!" by Robin Klein, permission granted by Haytul Pty. Ltd. Copyright © Curtis Brown (Aust) Pty. Ltd., Sydney.

"April Rain Song" from *The Dream Keeper and Other Poems* by Langston Hughes. Copyright 1932 by Alfred A. Knopf, Inc. and renewed 1960 by Langston Hughes. Reprinted by permission of the publisher.

"Arbor Day" from *Rhymes About Us* by Marchette Chute. Published by E. P. Dutton. Copyright 1974 by Marchette Chute. Reprinted by permission of Elizabeth Roach.

"Awakenings" from *Welcome and Other Poems* by Geoffrey Summerfield, published by Scholastic Publications Ltd., 1983.

"Baggage" from *Crickety Cricket! The Best-Loved Poems of James S. Tippett*. Copyright © 1933, copyright renewed © 1973 by Martha K. Tippett. Selection reprinted by permission of HarperCollins Publishers.

"A Band of Gorillas" from *A Bundle of Beasts* by Patricia Hooper. Text copyright © 1987 by Patricia Hooper. Reprinted by permission of Houghton Mifflin Co. All rights reserved.

"Beans, Beans, Beans" from *Hooray for Chocolate*, © 1960 by Lucia and James L. Hymes, Jr. Reprinted by permission of Addison-Wesley Publishing Company, Inc.

Acknowledgments

"The Bear" from *A Child's Bestiary.* Copyright © 1977 by Boskydell Artists Ltd. Reprinted by permission of Georges Borchardt, Inc. on behalf of the Estate of John Gardner.

"Between Birthdays" from *Custard and Company* by Ogden Nash. Copyright © 1961, 1962 by Ogden Nash. By permission of Little, Brown and Company.

"Bird-Noise" from *Welcome and Other Poems* by Geoffrey Summerfield, published by Scholastic Publications Ltd., 1983.

"Birthday Weather" Copyright © 1968, 1971 by Siv Widerberg. Translation © 1973 by Verne Moberg. From the book *I'm Like Me.* Published by The Feminist Press at The City University of New York. All rights reserved.

"Birthdays" from *Yellow Butter Purple Jelly Red Jam Black Bread* by Mary Ann Hoberman. Reprinted by permission of Gina Maccoby Literary Agency. Copyright © 1981 by Mary Ann Hoberman.

"Birthdays" from *Around and About* by Marchette Chute. Copyright 1957 by E. P. Dutton. Copyright renewed 1984 by Marchete Chute. Reprinted by permission of Elizabeth Roach.

"Blum" by Dorothy Aldis, reprinted by permission of G. P. Putnam's Sons from *Here, There and Everywhere,* copyright © 1927, 1928, copyright renewed © 1955, 1956 by Dorothy Aldis.

"Book Lice" from *Joyful Noise* by Paul Fleischman. Copyright © 1988 by Paul Fleischman. Selection reprinted by permission of HarperCollins Publishers.

"Books on the Prowl" by Rick Kilcup, courtesy of the author.

"Borders" from *All the Colors of the Race* by Arnold Adoff. Copyright © 1982 by Arnold Adoff. By permission of Lothrop, Lee & Shepard Books, a division of William Morrow & Company, Inc.

"Boring" from *What I Did Last Summer* by Jack Prelutsky. Copyright © 1984 by Jack Prelutsky. By permission of Greenwillow Books, a division of William Morrow & Company, Inc.

"A Boy and His Dog" from *Mud, Moon and Me* by Zaro Weil. Text copyright © 1989 by Zaro Weil. Reprinted by permission of Houghton Mifflin Company. All rights reserved.

"Brachiosaurus" from *Yellow Butter Purple Jelly Red Jam Black Bread* by Mary Ann Hoberman. Reprinted by permission of Gina Maccoby Literary Agency. Copyright © 1981 by Mary Ann Hoberman.

"Buggity" from *Near the Window Tree* by Karla Kuskin. Copyright © 1975 by Karla Kuskin. Selection reprinted by permission of HarperCollins Publishers.

"Burglar" from *Balloons and Other Poems* by Debra Chandra. Copyright © 1988 by Debra Chandra. Reprinted by permission of Farrar, Straus Giroux, Inc.

"By Myself" by Eloise Greenfield from *Honey, I Love and Other Poems.* Copyright © 1978. Published by HarperCollins Publishers.

"Caterpillar" Copyright © 1967 by Jack Prelutsky. Used by permission of author.

"Chameleon" by Alan Brownjohn. Used by permission of Rosica Colin Limited. Copyright Alan Brownjohn, 1970.

"Chocolate" from *Eats* by Arnold Adoff. Copyright © 1979 by Arnold Adoff. By permission of Lothrop, Lee & Shepard Books, a division of William Morrow & Company, Inc.

"Chocolate Cake" from *All Day Long* by Nina Payne, copyright © 1973 by Nina Payne.

"Coincidence" from *Long Ago in Oregon* by Claudia Lewis. Text copyright © 1987 by Claudia Lewis. Selection reprinted by permission of HarperCollins Publishers.

"The Color-Eater" reprinted with permission of Margaret K. McElderry Books, an imprint of Macmillan Publishing Company, from *I'm Going to Pet a Worm Today and Other Poems* by Constance Levy. Copyright © 1991 by Constance Kling Levy.

Acknowledgments

"Condensed Version" from *Hey World, Here I Am!* by Jean Little. Text Copyright © 1986 by Jean Little. Selection reprinted by permission of HarperCollins Publishers.

"Conversation" from *There Is No Rhyme for Silver* by Eve Merriam. Copyright © 1962 Eve Merriam. © renewed 1990 Eve Merriam. Reprinted by permission of Marian Reiner.

"Conversation Hearts" from *All the Day Long* by Nina Payne. Copyright © 1973 by Nina Payne. Used by permission of the author.

"Courage" by Emily Hearn from *Hockey Card and Hopscotch* by Emily Hearn and John McInnes. Copyright 1980. Used by permission of Nelson Canada, a division of Thomson Canada Limited.

"The Court Jester's Last Report to the King" by Jack Prelutsky from *The Sheriff of Rottenshot*, Copyright © 1982. By permission of Greenwillow Books, a division of William Morrow & Company, Inc.

"Cow's Complaint" from *Come On Into My Tropical Garden* by Grace Nichols, reproduced with permission of Curtis Brown Group Ltd., London on behalf of Grace Nichols. Copyright © Grace Nichols 1988.

"Coyotes" by Jon Whyte, by permission of Barbara Whyte.

"The Crocodile's Brushing His Teeth" from *Who's Been Sleeping in My Porridge?* by Colin McNaughton. First published in the United States by Ideals Publishing Corporation, 199, Nashville, Tennessee 37214. Copyright © 1990. Used by permission of Ideals Publishing Corporation.

"Crush" by Julie Fredericksen, by permission of the author.

"Dad and the Cat and the Tree" from *Rabbittin* by Kit Wright, published by HarperCollins Publishers Ltd. Used by permission of HarperCollins Publishers.

"December" by Sanderson Vanderbilt from *Creative Youth*, edited by Hughes Mearns. Copyright 1925 Doubleday. Used by permission of Doubleday, a division of Bantam Doubleday Dell Publishing Group, Inc.

"The Dog Lovers" from *Small Dreams of a Scorpion* by Spike Milligan (Michael Joseph, 1972) copyright © Spike Milligan Productions Ltd, 1972. Reproduced by permission of Michael Joseph Ltd.

"The Dog" from *Consider the Lemming* by Jeanne Steig. Verse copyright © 1988 by Jeanne Steig. Reprinted by permission of Farrar, Straus & Giroux, Inc.

"Dragon" from *Any Me I Want to Be* by Karla Kuskin. Copyright © 1972 by Karla Kuskin. Selection reprinted by permission of HarperCollins Publishers.

"Ebonee," from *Red Dog, Blue Fly* by Sharon Bell Mathis. Copyright © 1991 by Sharon Bell Mathis. Used by permission of Viking Penguin, a division of Penguin Books USA Inc.

"Elephant for Sale" by Maurice Poe from *Willie MacGurkle and Friends*, © 1987 Curriculum Associates, Inc. North Billerica, MA 01862, USA. Used by permission of Curriculum Associates, Inc.

"An Eraser" from *Just Beyond Reach and Other Riddle Poems* by Bonnie Larkin Nims. Copyright © 1992 by Barbara Larkin Nims. Reprinted by permission of Scholastic Inc.

"Ethel Earl" from *In the Garden of Bad Things* by Doug MacLeod, published by Penguin Books Australia, 1981. Used by permission of Penguin Books Australia.

"Extra! Extra!" from *Who's Been Sleeping in My Porridge?* by Colin McNaughton, first published in the United States by Ideals Publishing Corporation, 1990, Nashville, Tennessee 37214. Copyright © 1990 by Colin McNaughton. Used by permission of publisher.

"Feathers" by Joseph Bruchac, first published in *Cricket*. Reprinted by permission of the author.

"The first horses were made of sea foam" by David Day from *Aska's Animals* by Warabe Aska. Text by David Day. Copyright © Ill., 1991 by Warabe Aska. Text, 1991 by David Day. Used by permission of Bantam Doubleday Dell Books for Young Readers.

"Fish" from *Consider the Lemming* by Jeanne Steig. Verse copyright © 1988 by Jeanne Steig. Reprinted by permission of Farrar, Straus and Giroux, Inc.

"Fish" by Ivor Cutler from *Gangsters, Ghosts and Dragonflies*, compiled by Brian Patten. By permission of HarperCollins Publisher Ltd.

"Fishes' Evening Song" from *Whisperings and Other Things*, published by Alfred A. Knopf. Reprinted by permission of McIntosh and Otis, Inc.

"Fling Me a Rainbow" from *Wind, Sand, and Sky* (E. P. Dutton). Text copyright © 1976 by Rebecca Caudill. Granted by permission of Rebecca Jean Baker.

"The Fly" from *Everything Glistens and Everything Sings: New and Selected Poems* by Charlotte Zolotow, copyright © by Charlotte Zolotow. Reprinted by permission of Harcourt Brace & Company.

"Foul Shot" by Edward Hoey, reprinted with special permission granted by *Read* magazine, published by Weekly Corporation. Copyright © renewed 1990, 1962 by Weekly Reader Corporation.

"Fourth of July" from *Cold Stars and Fireflies: Poems of the Four Seasons* by Barbara Juster Esbensen. Copyright © 1984. Reprinted by permission of HarperCollins Publishers.

"The Gentleman Bookworm" Copyright © 1993 by J. Patrick Lewis. Used by permission of author.

"Giraffe" from *Laughing Time* by William Jay Smith. Copyright © 1980. Reprinted by permission of Farrar, Strauss & Giroux, Inc.

"The Girl Who Makes the Cymbals Bang" reprinted with permission of Margaret K. McElderry Books, an imprint of Macmillan Publishing Company, from *The Kite That Braved Old Orchard Beach* by X. J. Kennedy. Copyright © 1991 by X. J. Kennedy.

"The Gold-Tinted Dragon" from *Dogs & Dragons, Trees & Dreams* by Karla Kuskin. Copyright © 1980 by Karla Kuskin. Selection reprinted by permission of HarperCollins Publishers.

"Goldfish" from *Don't Ever Cross a Crocodile* by Kaye Starbird. Copyright © 1963 Kaye Starbird. Copyright renewed 1991 Kaye Starbird. Used by permission of Marian Reiner.

"Good Chew" reprinted with permission of Margaret K. McElderry Books, an imprint of Macmillan Publishing Company, from *Pigeon Cubes* and Other Verse, by N. M. Bodecker. Copyright © 1982 By N. M. Bodecker.

"Gourd, Have Mercy" from *Light-metres*, published 1982 by Everest House. Copyright © Felicia Lamport. Used by permission of author.

"Great Pitches" Copyright © 1993 by J. Patrick Lewis. Used by permission of author.

"Grocery Oasis" by Ruth Haq, originally appeared in *Cricket* Magazine, August 1993. Copyright © 1993 by Ruth Haq. Used by permission of author.

"Haircut" from *Bird Song* by Yoshiko Uchida. Reprinted by permission of the Estate of Yoshiko Uchida.

"Halfway Down" from *When We Were Young* by A. A. Milne. Copyright 1924 by E. P. Dutton, renewed 1952 by A. A. Milne. Used by permission of Dutton Children's Books, a division of Penguin USA Inc.

"Hands" by Bobbi Katz. Copyright © 1976 by Bobbi Katz. Used by permission of author.

"Handyman" by Homer Phillips reprinted with permission of *The Saturday Evening Post*.

"Happy Birthday Card" by Rony Robinson, reprinted by permission of the Peters Fraser & Dunlop Group Ltd.

"Happy Birthday, Dear Dragon" from *The New Kid on the Block* by Jack Prelutsky. Copyright © 1984 by Jack Prelutsky. By permission of Greenwillow Books, a division of William Morrow & Company, Inc.

"Happy Birthday Dilroy!" from *I Din Do Nuttin* by John Agard. Copyright © 1983. By permission of The Bodley Head.

Acknowledgments

"Harry the Hawk" reprinted with the permission of Margaret K. McElderry Books, an imprint of Macmillan Publishing Company from *Nonstop Nonsense* by Margaret Mahy. Copyright © 1977 Margaret Mahy.

"Here Comes the Band" by William Cole. Copyright © William Cole. Reprinted by permission of author.

"Holding Hands" by Lenore M. Link. Copyright © 1936 by Instructor Publications, Inc. First published in *St. Nicholas* magazine. Reprinted by permission of Scholastic, Inc.

"Homework" by Jane Yolen, reprinted by permission of Curtis Brown, Ltd. Copyright © 1981 by Jane Yolen.

"Homework" by Russell Hoban. Copyright © 1964 by Russell Hoban reprinted with the permission of Wylie, Aitken & Stone, Inc.

"Hot Line" by Louella Dunann reprinted with permission from *The Saturday Evening Post*.

"How Do You Say Goodbye?" from *Auntie's Knitting a Baby* by Lois Simmie. Copyright © 1984 by Lois Simmie. Reprinted with permission of the publisher, Orchard Books, New York.

"How to Assemble a Toy" from *Mummy Took Cooking Lessons* by John Ciardi. Text copyright © 1990 by Judith C. Ciardi. Reprinted by permission of Houghton Mifflin Company. All rights reserved.

"How to Tell the Top of the Hill" from *The Reason for the Pelican* by John Ciardi, 1959. Reprinted courtesy of the Ciardi Family Trust.

"I Had a Little Secret" from *Beneath A Blue Umbrella* by Jack Prelutsky. Text Copyright © 1990 by Jack Prelutsky. By permission of Greenwillow Books, a division of William Morrow & Company, Inc.

"I Hear the Usual Thump" from *In for Winter, Out for Spring* by Arnold Adoff. Copyright © 1991 by Arnold Adoff, reprinted by permission of Harcourt Brace & Company.

"I Wish I Could Wiggle My Nose" by Sharon Burstein. Copyright © by Sharon Burstein. Reprinted by permission of author.

"Ice Cream" by Rick Kilcup, reprinted by courtesy of the author.

"I'm Going to Pray for Peace," reprinted with permission of Macmillan Publishing Company from *Jenny* by Beth P. Wilson. Copyright © 1990 by Beth P. Wilson.

"Imaginary Room" from *Roomrimes* by Sylvia Cassedy. Text copyright © 1987 by Sylvia Cassedy. Reprinted by permission of HarperCollins Publishers.

"in Just-spring" is reprinted from *Complete Poems, 1904–1962*, by E. E. Cummings, edited by George J. Firmage, by permission of Liveright Publishing Corporation. Copyright © 1923, 1951, 1991 by the Trustees for the E. E. Cummings Trust.

"In the Cupboard" from *Over and Over Again* by Barbara Ireson, published by Hutchinson Children's Books. Permission by Random House UK Ltd.

"In the Museum" from *Everything Glistens and Everything Sings: New and Selected Poems* by Charlotte Zolotow, copyright © by Charlotte Zolotow, reprinted by permission of Harcourt Brace & Company.

"The Inventor Thinks Up Helicopters" reprinted with permission of Atheneum Publishers, an imprint of Macmillan Publishing Company, from *The Tigers Brought Pink Lemonade* by Patricia Hubbell. Copyright © by Patricia Hubbell.

"Jelly Beans" by Aileen Fisher. By permission of the author who controls all rights.

"Jenny the Juvenile Juggler" by Dennis Lee. Copyright © 1991 Dennis Lee. By permission of Sterling Lord Associates.

"Jigsaw Puzzle" by Russell Hoban. Copyright © 1970 by Russell Hoban reprinted with the permission of Wylie, Aitken & Stone, Inc.

"Just Simply Alive" by Issa from *Haiku*, published by the Hokuseido Press. Reprinted by permission of Hokuseido Press.

Acknowledgments

"Keep a Poem in Your Pocket" from *Something Special* by Beatrice Schenk de Regniers. Copyright © 1958 by Beatrice Schenk de Regniers. © renewed 1986. Reprinted by permission of Marian Reiner for the author.

"Kicking Up" by Jane Yolen reprinted by permission of Philomel Books from *Bird Watch*, text copyright © 1990 by Jane Yolen.

"Knoxville, Tennessee" from *Black Feeling, Black Talk, Black Judgment* by Nikki Giovanni. Copyright © 1968, 1970 by Nikki Giovanni. By permission of William Morrow & Company, Inc.

"The Last Day of School" from *What I Did Last Summer* by Jack Prelutsky. Copyright © 1984 by Jack Prelutsky. By permission of Greenwillow, Inc.

"Last-minute Change" by Tony Johnston, copyright © Tony Johnston, by permission of the author.

"Lazy Jane" text and art from *Where the Sidewalk Ends* by Shel Silverstein. Copyright © 1974 by Evil Eye Music, Inc. Selection reprinted by permission of HarperCollins Publishers.

"The Library Cheer" reprinted by permission of the author. Copyright © 1983 Garrison Keillor.

"The Limerick's Lively to Write" from *One at a Time* by David McCord. Copyright © 1961, 1962 by David McCord. By permission of Little, Brown and Company.

"Look Up!" from *Street Talk* by Ann Turner. Copyright © 1986 by Ann Turner. Reprinted by permission of Houghton Mifflin Company. All rights reserved.

"Magnet" from *More Small Poems* by Valerie Worth. Poems copyright © 1976 by Valerie Worth. Reprinted by permission of Farrar, Straus & Giroux, Inc.

"Message from a Caterpillar" from *Something New Begins* by Lilian Moore. Copyright © 1967, 1969, 1972, 1975, 1980, 1982, by Lilian Moore. Reprinted by permission of Marian Reiner for the author.

"Missing Mama" from *Nathaniel Talking* by Eloise Greenfield, published by Black Butterfly Children's Books, 1988. By permission of Marie Brown Associates.

"The Mitten Song" from *A Pocketful of Poems* by Mary Louise Allen. Copyright © 1957 by Marie Allen Howarth. Selection reprinted by permission of HarperCollins Publishers.

"Moon of the Falling Leaves" reprinted by permission of Philomel Books from *Thirteen Moons on Turtle's Back* by Joseph Bruchac and Jonathan London. Copyright © 1992 by Joseph Bruchac and Jonathan London.

"Mop and Broom" from *Do Not Feed the Table* by Dee Lillegard, Illustrated by Keiko Narahasi. Copyright © 1993 by Dee Lillegard, Illustrations © 1993 by Keiko Narahasi. Used by permission of Delacorte Press, a division of Bantam Doubleday Dell Publishing Group, Inc.

"Mosquitoes" from *Hey World, Here I Am!* by Jean Little. Text copyright © 1986 by Jean Little. Selection reprinted by permission of HarperCollins Publishers.

"Mother's Chocolate Valentine" from *It's Valentine's Day* by Jack Prelutsky. Copyright © 1983 by Jack Prelutsky. By permission of Greenwillow Books, a division of William Morrow & Company, Inc.

"The Muddy Puddle" by Dennis Lee. Copyright © 1977 Dennis Lee. Used by permission of Sterling Lord Associates.

"Mural on Second Avenue" reprinted with permission of Atheneum Publishers, an imprint of Macmillan Publishing Company, from *Something New Begins* by Lilian Moore. Copyright © 1982 by Lilian Moore.

"My Uncle Charlie" from *One Big Yo to Go*. Copyright © 1980 by Valerie Osborne. Published by Oxford University Press Australia, 1980. Used by permission of author.

"Neighbors" from *Bird Song* by Yoshiko Uchida reprinted by permission of the Estate of Yoshiko Uchida.

"The New Gnus" © John Foster 1991. Reprinted from *Four O'Clock Friday* by John Foster (1991) by permission of Oxford University Press.

Acknowledgments

"The New Kid" by Mike Makley. Courtesy of the author.

"No Difference" from *Where the Sidewalk Ends* by Shel Silverstein. Copyright © 1974 by Evil Eye Music, Inc. Selection reprinted by permission of HarperCollins Publishers.

"Numbers Game" from *All in Sport* by Richard Armour, copyright © 1972 by Richard Armour. Reprinted by permission of McGraw-Hill, Inc.

"Nutty Chocolate Cookies" from *Cricket's Cookery* by Pauline Watson and the Editors of *Cricket* Magazine. Copyright © 1977 by Random House, Inc. and Open Court Publishing Co. Reprinted by permission of Random House, Inc.

"Order" from *The Way Things Are and Other Poems* by Myra Cohn Livingston. Copyright © 1974 by Myra Cohn Livingston. Reprinted by permission of Marian Reiner for the author.

"Overdog" by Tony Johnston. Copyright © Tony Johnston, used by permission of the author.

"Packing Up," originally appeared in *Cricket* magazine, March 1994. By permission of Grace Cornell Tall.

"Padiddle" copyright © 1991 by J. Patrick Lewis. Used by permission of author.

"Paper Bag" from *Mud, Moon and Me* by Zaro Weil. Text copyright © 1989 by Zaro Weil. Reprinted by permission of Houghton Mifflin Company. All rights reserved.

"Passing Fair" from *The Sidewalk Racer and Other Poems of Sports and Motion* by Lillian Morrison. Copyright © 1965, 1967, 1968, 1977 by Lillian Morrison. Reprinted by permission of Marian Reiner for the author.

"Pencil and Paint" from *Eleanor Farjeon's Poems for Children*, originally appeared in *Joan's Door* by Eleanor Farjeon. Copyright 1926, 1954 by Eleanor Farjeon. Selection reprinted by permission of HarperCollins Publishers.

"Pencils" from *Who Shrank My Grandmother's House: Poems of Discovery* by Barbara Juster Esbensen. Copyright © 1992 by Barbara Juster Esbensen. Selection reprinted by permission of HarperCollins Publishers.

"People There Did Things" reprinted with the permission of Charles Scribner's Sons, an imprint of Macmillan Publishing Company from *The Best Town in the World* by Byrd Baylor. Copyright © 1982 Byrd Baylor.

"Peter Ping and Patrick Pong" by Dennis Lee. Copyright © 1991 by Dennis Lee. From the book *The Ice Cream Store* by Dennis Lee with illustrations by David McPhail. Published in Canada by HarperCollins Publishers Ltd. and in the United States by Scholastic Inc. Used by permission of HarperCollins Publishers Ltd.

"The Picture" from *The Butterfly Jar* by Jeff Moss. Copyright © 1989 by Jeff Moss. Used by permission of Bantam Books, a division of Bantam Doubleday Dell Publishing Group, Inc.

"Pigeons" from *Around and About* by Marchette Chute, copyright 1957 by E. P. Dutton. Copyright renewed 1984 by Marchette Chute. Reprinted by permission of Elizabeth Roach.

"The Pony on Halloween" reprinted with permission of Atheneum Publishers, an imprint of Macmillan Publishing Company, from *A Grass Green Gallop* by Patricia Hubbell. Copyright © 1990 by Patricia Hubbell.

"Popalong Hopcorn" from *Popcorn Pie* by Judith Nicholls, first published by Mary Glasgow Ltd., 1988. Used by permission of HarperCollins Publishers.

"Postman, Postman" from *Whiskers and Rhymes* by Arnold Lobel. Copyright © 1985 by Arnold Lobel. By permission of Greenwillow Books, a division of WIlliam Morrow & Company, Inc.

"President" by Dee Anderson, copyright © Dee Anderson. Courtesy of author.

"Purple" from *The Butterfly Jar* by Jeff Moss. Copyright © 1989 by Jeff Moss. Used by permission of Bantam Books, a division of Bantam Doubleday Dell Publishing Company, Inc.

Acknowledgments

"Purpose for Radishes" excerpt, from *Nice Deity* by Martha Baird (Definition Press, 1955).

"The Rabbit" by Alan Brownjohn. Reprinted be permission of Rosica Colin Limited. Copyright © Alan Brownjohn, 1983.

"Rain" from *Silly Verse for Kids* by Spike Milligan (Michael Joseph, 1984), copyright © Spike Milligan Productions Ltd., 1984. Reproduced by permission of Michael Joseph Ltd.

"Read to Me Riddles" from *The Three Bears Rhyme Book*, copyright © 1987 by Jane Yolen, reprinted by permission of Harcourt Brace Jovanovich, Inc.

"Reading is Dangerous" by Tony Johnston. Copyright © Tony Johnston. Used by permission of the author.

"A Red Morning Sky" by Issa from *Haiku*, published by the Hokuseido Press. Reprinted by permission of Hokuseido Press.

"A Remarkable Adventure" from *Something Big Has Been Here* by Jack Prelutsky. Copyright © 1990 by Jack Prelutsky. By permission of Greenwillow Books, a division of William Morrow & Company, Inc.

"remembering . . ." by Nikki Grimes, from *Something on My Mind* by Nikki Grimes, pictures by Tom Feelings. Copyright © 1978 by Nikki Grimes. Used by permission of Dial Books for Young Readers, a division of Penguin Boooks USA Inc.

"Rhyming the Rainbow" from *Cinnamon Seed* by John Travers Moore. Copyright 1967 by John Travers Moore, published by Houghton Mifflin Co. Used by permission of author.

"Rice Pudding" from *When We Were Very Young* by A. A. Milne. Illustrations by E. H. Shepard. Copyright 1924 by E. P. Dutton, renewed 1952 by A. A. Milne. Used by permission of Dutton Children's Books, a division of Penguin Books USA Inc.

"Roadside Peddlers" from *Not a Copper Penny in Me House* (1993) by Monica Gunning. By permission of Wordsong, an imprint of Boyds Mills Press.

"Sam at the Library" by Carol Combs Hole from *Jack and Jill* magazine, copyright © 1967 by The Curtis Publishing Company. Used by permission of Children's Better Health Institute, Benjamin Franklin Literary & Medical Society, Inc., Indianapolis, IN.

"School Concert" from *Rhymes About Us* by Marchette Chute. Published 1974 by E. P. Dutton. Copyright 1974 by Marchette Chute. Reprinted by permission of Elizabeth Roach.

"Seaside" from *Out and About* by Shirley Hughes. Copyright © 1988 by Shirley Hughes. By permission of Lothrop, Lee & Shepard Books, a division of William Morrow & Company, Inc.

"September Is" by Bobbi Katz. Copyright © 1978 Bobbi Katz. Used by permission of Bobbi Katz who controls all rights.

"Sheep" by Mike Thaler from *A Zooful of Animals*, published by Houghton Mifflin Company. Copyright © Mike Thaler, 1992. Used by permission of author.

"Sneeze" from *No One Writes a Letter to the Snail* by Maxine Kumin. Reprinted by permission of Curtis Brown, Ltd. Copyright © 1962 by Maxine Kumin. Copyright renewed.

"The Sneeze" from *Toes in My Nose* by Sheree Fitch. Copyright © 1987. Reprinted by permission of Doubleday Canada Limited.

"Soap Bubbles" from *Bird Song* by Yoshiko Uchida. Reprinted by permission of the Estate of Yoshiko Uchida.

"Somersaults and Headstands" from *Stilts, Somersaults, and Headstands* by Kathleen Fraser. Copyright © 1968 by Kathleen Fraser. Reprinted by permission of Marian Reiner for the author.

"Something Told the Wild Geese" by Rachel Field. Reprinted with permission of Macmillan Publishing Company, from *Poems* by Rachel Field. Copyright 1934 by Macmillan Publishing Company, renewed 1962 by Arthur S. Pederson.

Acknowledgments

"Song of the Pop-Bottlers" by Morris Bishop from *The Best of Bishop* (Cornell). Copyright © 1950, 1978 Alison Kingsbury Bishop. Originally in *The New Yorker*.

"Sorting Out the Kitchen Pans" from *All Join In* by Quentin Blake. Copyright © 1990 by Quentin Blake. By permission of Little, Brown and Company.

"Spelling Bee" reprinted with permission of Bradbury Press, an affiliate of Macmillan, Inc., from *Waiting to Waltz* by Cynthia Rylant. Copyright © 1984 by Cynthia Rylant.

"Squirrel" reprinted by permission of the Estate of Yoshiko Uchida.

"Squirrel" from *At the Top of My Voice and Other Poems* by Felice Holman. Copyright © by Felice Holman and Charles Scribner's Sons, publisher (1970). Used by permission of Valen Associates, Inc.

"The Sugar Lady" from *City Sandwich* by Frank Asch. Copyright © 1978 by Frank Asch. By permission of Greenwillow Books, a division of William Morrow & Company, Inc.

"Summer Storm" from *Wind, Sand, and Sky* (E. P. Dutton). Text copyright © 1976 by Rebecca Caudill. Granted by permission of Rebecca Jean Baker.

"Supermarket" from *At the Top of My Voice* by Felice Holman. Copyright © by Felice Holman and Charles Scribner's Sons, publisher (1970). Used by permission of Valen Associates, Inc.

"A Tale Told Standing" by Grace Cornell Tall. Used with permission of author.

"The Thanksgiving Mouse" by Grace Cornell Tall, first published in *Cricket, the Magazine for Children*, November 1991. Used by permission of Grace Cornell Tall.

"There was a young fellow named Hugh" from *Songs for My Dog and Other People* by Max Fatchen (Kestrel Books, 1980). Copyright © Max Fatchen, 1980. Used by permission of John Johnson (Authors' Agent) Limited, London.

"They Were My People" from *Come on into My Tropical Garden* by Grace Nichols, reproduced with permission of Curtis Brown Ltd, London on behalf of Grace Nichols. Copyright © Grace Nichols 1988.

"Thoughts on Talkers" from *The Collected Poems of Freddy the Pig* by Walter R. Brooks. Copyright © 1953 by Walter R. Brooks. Reprinted by permission of Alfred A. Knopf, Inc.

"To Catch a Fish" from *Under the Sunday Tree* by Eloise Greenfield. Text copyright © 1988 by Eloise Greenfield. Selection reprinted by permission of HarperCollins Publishers.

"Trinity Place" copyright © 1959 by Phyllis McGinley, from *Times Three* by Phyllis McGinley. Used by permission of Viking Penguin, a division of Penguin Books USA Inc.

"True" from *I Feel the Same Way* by Lilian Moore. Copyright © 1967 by Lilian Moore. Reprinted by permission of Marian Reiner for the author.

"The Turkey" from *A Child's Bestiary* by John Gardner. Copyright © 1977 by Boskydell Artists Ltd. Reprinted by permission of Georges Borchardt, Inc. on behalf of the Estate of John Gardner.

"Two People I Would Like to Be Like" from *If Only I Could Tell You* by Eve Merriam. Copyright © 1983 by Eve Merriam. Reprinted by permission of Marian Reiner.

"Unfair" by Bobbi Katz. Copyright © 1973 by Bobbi Katz who controls all rights. Used by permission of author.

"The Valentine" by Linda G. Paulsen. Used by permission of author.

"Valentines" by Aileen Fisher by permission of the author who controls all rights.

"Wake Up" from *Mud, Moon, and Me* by Zaro Weil. Text copyright © 1989 by Zaro Weil. Reprinted by permission of Houghton Mifflin Company. All rights reserved.

"Wearing of the Green" by Aileen Fisher reprinted by permission from *Holiday Programs for Boys and Girls*, copyright © 1953, 1980, by Aileen Fisher. Plays, Inc, Publishers, Boston, MA.

Acknowledgments

"What is Orange?" from *Hailstones and Halibut Bones* by Mary O'Neil and Leonard Weisgard, Ill. Copyright © 1961 by Mary LeDuc O'Neill. Used by permission of Doubleday, a division of Bantam Doubleday Dell Publishing Group, Inc.

"What Someone Said When He Was Spanked on the Day Before His Birthday" by John Ciardi, reprinted courtesy of the Ciardi Family Trust.

"Wheels, Wheels, Wheels" reprinted with permission of Macmillan Publishing Company from *Graham Cracker Animals 1–2–3* by Nancy White Carlstrom. Copyright © 1989 by Nancy White Carlstrom.

"Who'd Be a Juggler?" by Cicely Herbert. Copyright © Cicely Herbert 1978. Reprinted by permission of the author.

"Why Are All of These Flowers in Bloom?" from *Flower Moon Snow: A Book of Haiku* by Kazue Mizumura. Copyright © 1977 by Kazue Mizumura. Selection reprinted by permission of HarperCollins Publishers.

"Why Do Onions Make Us Cry?" from *Where Do Fish Go in Winter & Answers to Other Great Mysteries* by Amy Goldman Koss, copyright © 1987. Available from Price Stern Sloan, Ine. Publishers, Los Angeles, California, USA.

"Why Does Popcorn Pop?" from *Where Do Fish Go in Winter & Answers to Other Great Mysteries* by Amy Goldman Koss, copyright © 1987. Available from Price Stern Sloan, Inc. Publishers, Los Angeles, California, USA.

"Wild Day at the Shore" from *At the Top of My Voice* by Felice Holman. Copyright © Felice Holman, and Charles Seribner's Sons, publisher (1970). Used by permission of Valen Associates, Inc.

"The Wind is Like an Onion" by Liz Rosenberg, courtesy of the author.

"Windstorm in Brooklyn" by Tony Johnston reprinted by permission of G. P. Putnam's Sons from *I'm Gonna Tell Mama I Want an Iguana*, text copyright © 1990 by Tony Johnston.

"The Wizard Said" from *The Word Party* by Richard Edwards and John Lawrence, Illustrator. Copyright © 1986 by Richard Edwards. Used by permission of Delaeorte Press, a division of Bantam Doubleday Dell Publishing Group, Ine.

"Write a Limerick Now" from *One at a Time* by David McCord. Copyright © 1961, 1962 by David McCord. By permission of Little, Brown and Company.

"Write a Petition" Copyright © 1968, 1971 by Siv Widerberg. Translation © 1973 by Verne Moberg. From the book *I'm Like Me*. Published by The Feminist Press at The City University of New York. All rights reserved.

"Zeroing In" from *Oatmeal Mittens* by Diane Dawber, Borealis Press Ltd., 1987. Reprinted by permission of the publisher.

"The Zoo" from *City Sandwich* by Frank Asch. Copyright © 1978 by Frank Asch. By permission of Greenwillow Books, a division of William Morrow & Company, Inc.

Introduction

When my grandmother was a little girl, reciting poetry was an important part of a young lady's education. When my mother was young, she too recited poetry in school. She also took elocution lessons on a weekly basis, which included learning narrative poems by classic poets and reciting them for collected aunts, uncles, and other relatives.

My mother was forced to take many different lessons, since my grandmother considered it her duty not only to educate her children, but also to provide work for a varied collection of immigrant friends, neighbors, and acquaintances. Apparantly, everyone in the neighborhood had some sort of talent to sell. From her lessons, my mother gained many skills that she later considered useless. For instance, she earned a degree in Swedish-American cooking. Obviously, this might have been transferred into the useful list. However, although she attended the classes, she must not have passed them all. The only dish my mother could cook was beef stew (which neither my father or I liked).

Her memories of most of these extracurricular classes were unpleasant and she vowed not to force any lessons on *her* child when she had one.

Poor Mom. She got herself a daughter who loved lessons and was always begging for more. One of my favorite classes, after horseback riding and ice skating, of course, was a Wednesday afternoon class in drama which included the oral interpretation of poetry. Although we had to memorize each poem perfectly and said each poem over and over and over till we were as perfect as the teacher thought we could be, I still loved the class, especially since we practiced on a real stage with stage lighting.

And then there was school. I did not always love poetry in school, especially when we were asked to identify the forms of poetry or write a specific type on demand.

For a time I attended a highly regarded, academically rigorous private school.

One of the most agonizing assignments I recall required each student in kindergarten through grade twelve to write a poem with the exact same title. The best poems were selected to be included in the school's literary magazine and the poets were given awards at an assembly. I never tried to win a prize. I just wanted to complete the assignment. One particularly dreadful year the subject was "round." It was a nice open-ended title, certainly not threatening, but I stamped my feet and audibly groaned whenever my mother passed anywhere near where I was struggling with "round." I must have turned something in, because I did graduate—certainly not with honors—from that school.

Observing children when I was a school and later a public librarian, I have been unhappy with many of the curricular strands that feature poetry. In many cases poetry is "taught" by writing poetry. I applaud the idea of writing poetry. If children begin early fashioning words into poetic forms, they will not end up groaning in high school over assignments like the one that still haunts me. However, the thing that distresses me is that we often expect our children to experiment with haiku, cinquains and such without first being introduced to the joys of appreciating poetry's varied rhythms. Although we advocate modeling for many activites, we often forget to show children our own delight in the poetry written by contemporary and traditional poets.

We can't really expect children to attempt the writing of a poem without introducing them to this art in a pleasurable manner. It's tempting to think that poetry belongs to a gentler, slower-paced society. One pictures girls in flouncy white dresses and boys in short pants and crisp white shirts listening to a begowned mother reading from a Victorian picture book. Today, in that same photo we might picture Mom and her children all wearing jeans and staring at a television screen. But, we can reconstruct the old tintype by visualizing Mom or one of the children sharing a poem.

If children are pressed for time, so are their parents, teachers, and librarians. Perhaps you'd like to take a crack at poetry, but are reluctant to take the time to search for appropriate poems. You are certain that there is no time left in an already crowded day to introduce poetry. Here is a collection of poems chosen just for the person who wants a ready reference to poems for elementary-school children with some ideas to help you present poetry quickly, every day. A collection of children's poems for adults, this book is designed to be used in conjunction with a successful project called the "poetry break."

I have introduced the poetry break in seminars in the United States and at conferences and international schools around the world. I know that it is being used in school and libraries and has been introduced in other situations such as day care centers, city councils and even in a correctional facility. Much of the idea's popularity may stem from the fact that the preparation is minimal and the actual presentation takes less than a minute from the structured activities of the day.

It only takes a sentence to describe the concept of the poetry break, but the applications of the idea are detailed in the following section for those who would like some advice on implementing the project on a building-wide basis.

PART ONE

THE POETRY BREAK

1

What the Poetry Break Is

It's easy. It's quick. It's effective. Essentially, someone walks around your building with a sign and a poem. He or she pops into each classroom, office, or department and calls out: "Poetry break!" Everyone in the room looks up, a poem is read aloud or recited. The listeners return to their activities, the poetry person continues to the next room. Here's how you do it.

You need:

    a sign
    a presenter
    a poem

How to:

Ask for volunteers to be the poetry people. Who? Administrators, staff and faculty members, children, young adults, parents, and other library patrons. Anyone who is willing should be welcomed.

Explain the program at a staff meeting so that everyone understands that at any time during the day, a poetry presenter might appear to present a poem. If some do not want to participate in the program on any given day, or not at all, they may post a sign on the door that says, "No poetry today, please." Undoubtedly, there will be at least one misanthrope in your institution who will not want this sort of disturbance in her or his room or office. Don't worry. When they see how little time it takes and how much everyone enjoys it, they just might capitulate and become strong supporters of the idea of the poetry break.

If you have a large group of willing volunteers you may want to hold a meeting—call it a reception or party to be sure that everyone remembers to come—to explain the procedure. If there are only a handful of presenters involved , you can tell them over a glass of milk or a cup of coffee in the lounge. The poetry people are special and should be treated with respect and appreciation.

Welcoming the Poetry Break Volunteers

You might incorporate some of the following points into your words of welcome and orientation to your new group:

"Welcome to the poetry troupe. You have been chosen (emphasize chosen even though they might have been coerced into volunteering this first time) to introduce the joys and wonders of poetry to our library patrons (or class, cub scout troop, etc.).

We will be touring the school (or library or mall) every day. You may go as individuals or with a partner. When you have a few minutes, pick up the poetry break sign and go to each classroom in the building. When you arrive at a classroom take a look at the door in case a notice has been posted saying, 'No poetry today please.' This sign will be on the door if the leader feels that an interuption, even for poetry, is inappropriate that day. If there is no sign, knock on the door, open it and announce, 'Poetry break'. As you walk to the front of the room the children and the adults will have a few seconds to adjust to your presence. Put the poetry break sign on the floor or desk while you read or recite, as you will want attention paid to the words of the poem and, if you are using a prop, you will need your hands to manipulate it.

The most important components of the poetry break are choosing a poem that you like and practicing reading or reciting it."

Choosing Poems

This book should provide you with numerous selections from which to choose some favorites, so browse through it or read it from cover to cover until you find a poem that pleases you. You can read directly from the book, or copy the poem so that others may use the book. When presenting, place the poem inside a folder or glue it onto poster board to give a more professional look. Pulling a ragged piece of paper from your pocket is a bit déclasée.

If you are a teacher or a school librarian, you may feel that it is important, even necessary, to find a poem that relates to the school curriculum. Please think of the poetry break as a separate, extracurricular activity. If you are impelled to tie a poem into the day's lesson plan this idea will fizzle because it will take too much of your time to find appropriate poems every day. There is no need to force everything into the study of the Civil War or photosynthesis. In fact, a poem might be remembered simply because it was different from the activities of a particular day or week.

Similarly, there is no need to find a poem for each age group that you visit. The idea is to make this project as easy to implement as possible. You will want to take just one poem throughout your institution on any given day. If your school or library caters to children from preschool to grade twelve it would take an inordinate amount of time to find a poem for each classroom or department that you are visiting each day. This means that one day you will be presenting a poem for young children and perhaps another day for older children. Everyone in the building gets a chance to hear all the poems. Eventually, the entire community will have heard all the poems in this book.

At School

An obvious and convenient occasion for a daily poetry break is during the school day. Once the staff understands that the poetry break will not be disruptive and will fulfill multiple needs, they will welcome this brief, but revitalizing interruption.

Try to avoid actually scheduling a time for the poetry break, as that will lock the presenters into a designated time which may sometimes end up being inconvenient for them and for the listeners. After all, since this activity only takes a few seconds from actual classtime, it would be more expedient to pick up the poetry break sign and walk through the school whenever the presenter has a few minutes.

The poetry break will work for any age group. You may find that the elementary-school staff is more amenable to the idea than the more structure-minded teachers who work with middle- and high-school students. However, they too, will see that the poetry break adds to rather than detracts from their busy school day.

Involve as many people in the poetry break as you can. The search for the daily poem often involves reading many poems until the perfect one is found which adds to the poetry experience. Children will enjoy the responsibility of walking through the halls, offices, and classrooms with an important errand. Teachers and administrators will find that they learn from being in all the classrooms in the school. And, it will be interesting for adults to observe the different reactions to the same poem in each classroom.

Classrooms are not the only place in the school to give a poetry break. Start each assembly with a poem. Preface all announcements with poetry. Use the school intercom for a poetry break. Even the school bus might be a good place for a poetry break. And don't forget to send each child home with a printed poem to share with their families.

Any place and any method of presentation will work if you are dedicated to keeping focused on the idea.

School and Community Boards

Attending an important meeting of the school board, the library commission, or the church elders? Bring your poetry break sign and a poem. Select something that you like, no need for it to relate in any way to the subject to be discussed.

In the Public Library

Naturally, you will want to initiate a poetry break at the public library. The children's room is the obvious place to begin, but consider the entire library as a stage for the presentation of poetry. If you have a large reference room, you may not want to disturb the more serious patrons, but you can experiment with the idea at non-peak periods and see if there are more people who enjoy the idea than are disturbed by it. In any case, the poetry break can be considered at the entrance of the library as a promotion idea. It may encourage the circulation of poetry volumes.

The outreach program is perfect for the poetry break idea. Any time a library staff member comes in contact with the public he or she can think, "Maybe this would be a good time to whip out a poem." Certainly, if you are exhibiting at a community fair or mall, the poetry break would give you an opportunity for brief effective programming to promote library services.

Church and Club Meetings

Explore the idea of introducing the poetry break to Saturday and Sunday schools as well as club meetings. You may feel that you should present a poem with an ecumenical slant, but this is not always necessary. You are trying to expand the poetry knowledge of your listeners, and if you choose a poem that seems appropriate for the group and setting, you'll most likely be demonstrating that poetry can be uplifting and inspirational.

3

Methods of Presentation

Reading Poetry Aloud

The whole idea of this book is to take the intimidation out of poetry, so it would be inappropriate to begin by giving you rules and regulations regarding reading poetry aloud. A few suggestions and hints may be in order, however, since poetry looks different than the narratives that are generally read to children.

Make sure that you give the title of the poem and the author. It is best to do this before *and* after the poem. You will want your audience to know and remember that poetry is written by real people, and that, if they like that poet, they can seek out more of his or her work.

Most likely, you will often read directly from the book. You will want your listeners to know that poetry comes from print and is written down for all to share.

Feel free to repeat a poem immediately. If it is worth hearing once, it should be worth hearing again. Poetry is like a good piece of music. Your enjoyment and understanding increases each time you hear it. You may also want to offer the same poem several times, at different poetry breaks and even read with different presenters, as the more your listeners hear a piece, the better will be their understanding of it and the deeper their reactions to it.

Poems are often only a verse or two long, and therefore, every word counts. When you are reading a longer narrative, you may be able to get away with glossing over a word you don't understand or slurring a word or two. When you read poetry, make sure that you distinctly articulate each word.

If the poem has a rhyming construction, you may find yourself so caught up in the rhythm that there is a danger of offering the poem in a singsong manner.

Rhymes give a lilting feeling to poetry, but there is no need to over emphasize the meter.

Make sure that you know the meaning of each word in the poem and how to pronounce all the words. Don't guess. You may be imparting the wrong meaning to the entire poem, and worse as the presenter you will "teach" your listeners the wrong pronunciation as well. As a young storyteller I often told Ruth Sawyer's "the Flea." The story contains several Spanish words. In one part of the story, the young shepherd arrives at the King's castle to try his luck at answering a riddle that has eluded far more educated men. The guards at the palace pass the young man from guard to guard saying "pobrecito." In my ignorance of Spanish, I thought that surely they were announcing him to the next person and at first I shouted the word as though I were the butler. Luckily, before I actually told the story I asked someone how to pronouce the word. It turned out that the guards were actually shaking their heads and intoning, "poor thing." Imagine how ridiculous I would have felt if I hadn't taken the time to find out the true meaning of the word. (Incidentally, the person I asked for help was a colleague of mine at the New York Public Library. Since I had approached him with my question he felt less shy and asked me to dinner. So, asking a question to sharpen your storytelling skills may get you a dinner date!)

Poets generally use standard punctuation. Look at the poem to see where the commas and periods are placed. They will tell you when to pause and stop just the way they do in stories or articles. This seems like an obvious thing to point out, but since poetry does look different on the page, it can be tempting to ignore the signals you're used to in other forms of oral reading.

You may find conversation in poetry. This is your chance to perform in a mini-play. When we read stories aloud that contain conversation, we often omit the "he says" and "she wondered" because our changes in voice, no matter how slight, will give the listener indication of who is speaking. You can't do that with poetry; you must read every word. To maintain the form of a poem, it may not be amended or it becomes unbalanced.

The tone or subject of a poem will further guide you in your oral presentations. If the poem is funny you will want to use a lighter tone than if the poem is serious. One word of caution: Just because a poem is about the loss of a pet or death does not mean that you must present it in a grim or lugubrious manner. Let the words tell the listeners what to feel. You don't need to signal a sad poem by bringing out a handkerchief—or smelling salts.

Try not to be so tied to the book that you fail to look up and physically share the poem. If you glance up into the eyes of your listeners they and you will feel more involved.

Recitation and Memorization

If you decide not to read a poem it's obvious that the alternate way to present the poem orally is to memorize it. Some adults and most children can do this easily. However, to require you or one of your volunteers to memorize before presenting may lessen the chances that the poetry break becomes a permanent, daily part of programming in your institution simply because it takes too much time and effort.

One of the easiest methods of memorizing a poem is to use it one day in the poetry break. If you are in a school with twelve classrooms or more, by the time you have made your way through half of the school, you undoubtedly will have memorized the poem. Now, you can use it another time and will already know the poem.

Knowing the words, of course, is not enough. After the words have been committed to memory, you still have to work on your delivery. As above, think in terms of the tone of the selection. Practice your recitation with a live audience. Perhaps you can find a willing friend or even a reluctant spouse to listen and give comments. I sometimes joke about practicing on my dog. At least with a pet, you are talking to a living creature rather than trying to recreate the performance feeling in the vacumn of a deserted kitchen or living room.

Another way of practicing is to tape yourself and listen to how you sound, critiquing your performance. An audio tape can serve another function, too, as it can help with the memorization. Hearing a poem over and over will be like listening to the words of a song. You will learn it through repetition.

If you would like to try reciting, but feel anxious about forgetting the words, why not take a copy of the poem with you and slip it into your pocket or place a book mark in the book so that you can open the book and easily find the poem if you get stuck. This may give you the security you need to help you through the first memorized presentation. After all, one of the reasons you are presenting poetry is to give your audience, the children, the knowledge that all those wonderful poems that they have been listening to come from books. If they see you carrying a book and referring to print it will reinforce the idea "poetry comes from books."

Take every opportunity to use your newly memorized poem so that it will become embedded in your memory and can be used whenever needed.

Once you and your volunteers have a reportoire of poems, you can tour outside your own facility with an entire program of memorized poems which will seem more professional to an outside audience.

Standing or Sitting

There is no rule that dictates whether you stand or sit while presenting. In fact, it would probably be advantageous to vary your presentations by standing one time and sitting the next. If you want the distance of formality, or if the group is large and everyone may not be able to see you if you're sitting, stand. If you want to have a more intimate, relaxed mood with a smaller group, sit. I would think that the choice of poem and its tone also might dictate the stance you take.

If you are using actions or a prop, you will probably want the physical flexibility that standing gives you.

Introducing the Poem

The easiest introduction of all is to use the poetry break framework. To focus the group's attention on you, simply say, "Poetry Break," and give the author and title of the poem.

A fuller introduction can precede the poem when you have time and feel it would be relevant. In fact, this is your chance to get in a little information without overshadowing the poem itself. For instance, you may want to talk about the poet who wrote the poem or about the topic. However, if your introduction is too involved you run the risk of having the introduction run longer than the poem itself, creating a sense of letdown.

Personal introductions work well, too. Tell the audience how you felt when you first read the poem or how it effected you later or why you chose this particular poem for them that day.

Despite the fact that I find it difficult to memorize poetry, a line from a poem I've read or heard will surface as I'm walking on the beach or watching a game. When I get home, I find myself searching through my poetry books so that I can reread the whole poem and enjoy it again. Sharing the kinds of connections poetry makes for you encourages your listeners to welcome poetry as an enriching, pleasurable part of all their activities, too.

Examples of personal introductions are provided in the Think About It section (pages 115–129) to get you started.

Add a little theater to your poetry routine by investing in a portable microphone, available at electronic stores, to introduce the poetry break. Deborah Peal, a Dade County, Florida, Teacher of the Year, uses this with children and adults in her school. The children beg to be poetry break volunteers, so that they can use the microphone.

Sharing a Poem

Choral reading was popular when my mother was a young girl. It is making a comeback in whole language classrooms. The idea is to recite poetry as a group. In the past, lines or verses were assigned to several voices rather like a singing chorus. Children auditioned and were grouped according to whether they had high or low voices. Lengthy rehearsal periods aimed at performance perfection.

Today our emphasis is on shared enjoyment. There may not be the time to bring a piece to peformance level, but your group can have fun trying.

Act It Out

Some poems work well if they are acted out. Conversation in the poem will help you to determine how many parts should be assigned. A single reader can also act out the selection. Use the poem as the script of a skit. Try not to overshadow the words of the poem with distracting actions. The action should follow and express the text. Here is a case in which you should memorize the poem. It's hard to mime playing basketball while you are trying to read from a book.

Mother Goose: An Introduction to Poetry

E. D. Hirsch, Jr., in his book *Cultural Literacy: What Every American Needs to Know* (Houghton Mifflin, 1987), suggested that there is a body of knowledge that all Americans need to know to function as literate citizens. The rhymes of Mother Goose have traditionally been a part of the common heritage of children growing up in America, no matter what their ethnic background.

It is true that other parts of the world have their own children's nursery rhymes, and some of these have traveled to this land with immigrants as part of their home culture, but the rhythmic nursery rhymes that originated in the British Isles form the basis of our traditional baby and preschool lore.

We are now making efforts to preserve the endangered species of the animal world; we may soon have to take organized action to preserve the childhood tradition of nursery rhymes. Children starting school today are more likely to be conversant with the exploits of the current cartoon characters on film and television than with the adventures of Humpty Dumpty.

Is Mother Goose worth introducing to those children who do not know these rhymes? Yes. Mother Goose is the perfect way to introduce children to rhyme and rhythm, readying them to listen easily and naturally to other forms of poetry. The familiary of the rhymes to those who heard them as toddlers will be comforting and bring back gentle memories. Those children who aren't aware of the rhymes, including children for whom English is a brand new language, will find them easy to learn and have fun playing with the lilting rhythm.

If you've forgotten the words to some of these rhymes of early childhood, you'll find a selection of favorites on pages 264–275. Slip one into the poetry break on a regular basis or occasionally present a short program of several well-loved Mother Goose rhymes.

Puppets and Poetry

Do you have a favorite puppet? He, she, or it may be the perfect person/thing to present poetry. A puppet can recite the poetry, or it can model appreciative listening, applauding at the end of the recitation.

Prop Poetry

To vary your presentation, now and then, you may want to experiment with visuals. Think in terms of using artifacts, illustrations, and even kitchen utensils. You'll find some specific suggestions to get you started on pages 94–114.

Poetry Break Sign

The poetry break sign is an important part of the poetry break since it visually clues your listeners to the fact that the folks at the door of the classroom, library, or office are there to entertain with a poem and not give a speech on dental hygiene.

The sign itself can be made by the children who will be the presenters. If they don't have the time, use an existing poster or picture and simply letter "Poetry Break" on it with a felt-tip pen. The sign does double duty if you glue a clear pocket to the back of your sign. You can buy clear acetate at a hardware store, or use a mylar book jacket cut down to a rectangle that will hold a sheet of paper. Insert the daily poem in the pocket so that it can be read easily while holding up the sign. The pocket is also handy for storing future choices or extra poems to use for "encores."

Almost anything works—from a professionally-painted sign to a recycled envelope. Once your poetry break is well established in your building you might consider a more permanent sign. Think about a stand that can be placed on a desk or the floor freeing the hands to use a prop or demonstrate an action.

Poetry Cards

Create a miniature poetry break sign and reproduce the design on index cards to distribute randomly to children throughout your building. When a child receives a card, they must choose and recite a poem. The recipient then passes the card along.

Buttons and Badges

You might want to provide buttons or badges that poetry break volunteers can wear when they are offering a poem, and wear proudly around the community, too, to pique interest in the project. Make them nice and large so that everyone will instantly recognize them as members of the poetry troupe.

Poetry Displays and Exhibits

Blitz your institution with printed poetry. Place copies of poems wherever you think people will be looking. Once you have a number of poems ready to post you can switch their location so that if someone missed the poem on the door frame, they may catch it on the back of the lavatory door. This keeps your display fresh without having to re-create it every time you want to use new material.

Doors

A door is an excellent location to display a poem, whenever you turn the door knob you are forced to see the poem posted there. Keep your door poetry short for a quick read and change the selection often.

Table-tops

Entertain your children with selected poetry readings affixed to desk tops, cafeteria tables and library tables. Use a roll of masking tape that will remove easily without damaging the surface. Encourage children to "steal" a poem if they would like to take it home to treasure. It helps to have some sort of graphic on the poetry sheet to catch the eye of the casual viewer.

Bulletin Boards

Post poems on bulletin boards or directly onto classroom and corridor walls with removable tape.

Bookmarks

Bookmarks may not always be used to keep your reading place in a book, but they certainly make nice carry-away souvenirs. Print poetry on colored stock to tuck into book bags, pockets, or desks.

Athletic Equipment

Take a walk to the gym or baseball field. Place a few poems on the bench in the dugout. It can be boring waiting for your turn to play. Reading, or maybe even memorizing, a poem will make the time go faster. Don't be surprised if the third baseman or -woman comes to the library asking for "more poems, please."

Chalkboard

Put a poem of the day on the chalkboard. Vary the subjects, poets, and location of the poem. If it always appears in the same place each new poem may not be read by everyone. Poetry aficionados will find it wherever it is placed.

Poetry Break Logo

To identify elements of the poetry break, think about using a logo that instantly means, "There's one of those poetry pieces again." The logo can be used on poems that are displayed throughout the institution and on the poetry break sign. The logo can adorn a T-shirt or be used as the masthead for a Poetry News sheet. Use one of these or design your own.

4

Poetry Activities

Poetry News

Start a news sheet that is distributed periodically, whenever there is time to create one. Use one of the poems in this book or one that children have written and feature it in an *Extra! Extra! Read All About It!* paper. Featuring one poem by simply reproducing it will remind readers that you really can keep a poem in your pocket. Whenever there are a few minutes, between classes, waiting for the bell to ring, waiting for Dad to pick them up at the library, they can read the newspaper and relish the words and rhythm of a poem. Leave a space on the sheet for readers to jot down reactions to the selections. Maybe they will be inspired to write their own poetry.

Letters to Poets

Write an admiring letter to your favorite poet. No need to mail it, as the poet may no longer be living or may not welcome a letter, even a fan letter, from a stranger. Post the admiring letter with the poem.

Puzzle Poetry

Duplicate poems onto poster board. Decorate them with designs. Cut them up to make pocket-puzzles. Put the pieces for each puzzle-poem in an envelope. Distribute the envelopes to the group. When the children have all reassembled their puzzles, each child shares her selection out loud.

16

Object Poetry

Collect pictures, toys, objects that represent particular poems. Have a copy of each of the poems displayed on a table. Children match the object with the poem and read it aloud.

Words

Choose a different word in a number of poems. Make a separate card for each word. Distribute the words, one to each child. The object is to read through the poems to find the magic word. When the poems have been matched with the words, they are shared aloud.

Tape a Poem

Children may want to choose a poem, practice reading it aloud and then, using an audio or video tape, they can record poems to listen to individually or as a group.

A taped poem would also be a thoughtful present to give to Mom or Dad or a grandparent. Hearing their voices on audio tapes or watching themselves on video can also help children—and adults—to fine-tune their deliveries and improve their presentations of poetry.

Vote a Poem

Once you have listened to a number of poems, you may want to hold an election for your group's favorite poem. Allow children to campaign for their choice. Election speeches could include the reading of other poems by the poet and background information on the poet's life.

Before the announcement of the winner is made, make sure that all the poems are heard several times by the group, recited or read by those who nominate.

Package Poetry

Gather objects and key them to poems to create pass-around exhibits. Miniatures that children are so fond of collecting are perfect for putting into individual boxes along with a copy of the poem. Examples are small glass or china animals exhibited with appropriate animal poems; coins to accompany poems about money; and common desk items, such as paper clips, erasers, or pencils, that poets have written about.

Poetry boxes can be passed around the room for all to enjoy or left on a table or bookshelf to peruse when children have a few minutes to read and examine the object.

Poster Poetry

You or your children can put poems on posters and exhibit them in the halls or on bulletin boards. The text of the poems should be in print big enough to see from afar. However, if your lettering skills are not good and you don't have access to a lettering machine of some sort, the poem can be duplicated from the book at the largest possible magnification, and a colorful drawing can be added to the poster. Your hope will be that the picture will attract people to the poster, so that they can read the poem.

Picture Presentations

It would be interesting to suggest that several children draw pictures illustrating the same poem to show the diversity of interpretation.

The drawings can then be used to illustrate poems for the poetry break. The artist holds the picture for the group to see while he or another person recites the poem. Those who are not very good at memorization can read the poem which has been written on the back of the picture or pictures.

It is not always necessary for the artist to be the presenter. One person can give the title of the poem, the poet's name and the artist's name, another can hold the artwork and a third can read the poem. In this way the art is viewed in context instead of just exhibited on the usual bulletin board.

Candle Poetry

The fire marshall will not like this idea, but it is an effective way of creating a romantic atmosphere for the poetry break and creates a ceremonial mood. The room is darkened. As each presenter comes to the front of the room, he or she lights a candle and proceeds to read or recite. The candles can remain lit until the group has finished, or each candle can be snuffed out at the end of each selection.

The candles should be in sturdy candle holders, both as a safety measure and to free the presenters' hands to gesture.

Flashlight Poetry

As a dramatic variation of the candle poetry above, turn off all the lights. As you enter the darkened room, you say the magic words, "Poetry Break." Turn on a flashlight and illuminate the page from which you are reading.

Music

Use recorded music or live renditions to introduce your poetry breaks. You might even have your own theme music just like a talk show host or disc jockey. If you are considering using music as a background to your reading aloud, it must be soft and unobtrusive, simply enhancing the mood the poem creates, or you run the danger of having the music overwhelm the words.

If you are traveling from room to room in a school or library, you can carry a small tape recorder with you, but make sure that it doesn't have a tinny sound or can be heard by only a select few in the front of the room, or you will defeat your ambition of presenting the poem in a classy and professional manner.

Guest Poetry

Invite a friend or community worker (policeperson, the mayor, the library director) to read her or his favorite poem. If someone would like to volunteer, but doesn't have a particular favorite, let him browse through this collection for inspiration.

Many literate adult readers have never actually read poetry aloud and many more have never appeared before children. Your guest might need your guidance in selecting and reading the poem to make this a pleasurable experience for everyone.

For a book week celebration, one school invited adults to come and read to the children. I was present when a well-known basketball star read before an eager third-grade class. He had chosen a story that he remembered reading as a child. It was a short story, by adult standards, but endless for excited eight-year-olds.

Indeed, it was the sort of story you would remember if you read it when you were in high school, but just not a good selection for thirty-two restless third graders. Actually, it probably didn't matter what that athlete read, as the children were awestruck that he was actually in their school library. And, at least he appeared to them to be a reader and that made the visit worthwhile. That guest may not have asked for help in choosing a selection, but if he had and had been aided by the school librarian, who was quite attuned to her students and knowledgeable about books, the session might have been even more memorable and enjoyable.

Selecting a poem to read aloud is easier if you have a favorite anthology, and perhaps this one can help present choices. I'm not suggesting that guests should not be allowed to read their own favorites, as obviously, it is preferable if a guest brings a poem that he likes, loves, or adores. One of the premises of the poetry break is that it doesn't matter if a poem is age appropriate or fits the curriculum. What matters is that children are introduced to the idea of poetry and to some of the very best examples of it.

Parent or Community Program

Children who have been participating in the poetry break will be having such fun that they will want to find a new and equally appreciative audience. Parents will be entertained and impressed if they experience a poetry break at a back-to-school night. Don't feel that everyone in a class or story group has to participate. If you make a big production of it—rehearsals, special poems, costumes—you may end up deciding it's all too much trouble and not attempt what could be a very simple and effective demonstration.

After you have tried this idea with parents, spread the talent throughout the community. Consider visiting a senior citizen or recreation center. Your poetry troupe can give a poetry break in the common room or if permission is obtained from the center's administration, they can stroll through the halls and entertain with the sounds of poetry.

Poetry Remembered

Have your children interview their families to determine what they recall as their favorite poems as children. Grandparents who may have been raised with little television may even have stronger memories of beloved poems.

20

Collect your discoveries in a presentation book, illustrated by the children. Distribute the poems in the community or display the choices in your library or classroom.

Foreign Language Poetry

Do you speak a foreign language, or do you know someone who does? Invite them to recite or read in their own language. No need to translate word for word, as a simple introduction summarizing the poem is enough. It will be interesting for chidren to hear how a concept is expressed in another language and at the same time to listen to the rhythm and rhyme of a piece in that language. If the language uses another alphabet such as Thai, Russian, or Arabic, it might be interesting for your children to see the poem in print.

Another way of offering poetry in other languages is to have two presenters, with one person offering the poem in English after it is heard in a foreign language. Then, repeat the poem again in the foreign language.

Reader's Theater and Poetry

Choose two or three players to read a poem aloud. Duplicate the poem for each of the readers. Highlight the lines that each will recite. The poems should be affixed to a folder with the poetry logo on the cover. This makes a more professional looking presentation. March into the room together and line up in front of the audience. Count a silent one, two, three. Open the folders and read aloud.

Poetry Recitation Contest

It's an old-fashioned idea that is just as viable today as it was in my grandmother's time. Put on a poetry recitation contest. Once again, it need not be elaborate. Simply announce that prizes—they can be inexpensive souvenirs or homemade certficates—will be awarded to the winners in the contest. Each participant chooses a poem she would like to learn and memorizes it. Each entrant should be encouraged to practice reciting with expression before the day of the contest. In this way, they will learn the poem not just for the single day of the competition, but they will remember it for years, even when they have children of their own. It's all right for several children to choose the same poem, but during the actual contest, those with the same poems should be alternated with different poems, just for variety and also so that comparisons are not quite so apparent.

Who wins? The person who makes you want to run home and learn the poem yourself. Watch for eye contact, clarity, expression and tone. This is not so much a contest of oral interpretation as a vehicle for a wider distribution of poetry.

Poetry Sleep-Over

Invite children to a poetry sleep-over. Children bring their sleeping bags to the library or community room. Everyone takes turns sharing poetry between feasting on pizza and listening to music. Who is invited? It depends on how much space you have. If your space is limited, you may want children to earn the right to come to the sleep-over. One librarian reported that she required children to memorize a poem every month. After they had successfully recited ten poems, they were invited to the culminating activity, the sleep-over.

The poems were chosen by the librarian and had to be recited perfectly to earn the privilege of an invitation to the sleep-over. The first year, although the poem of the month was posted early in the school year, few people came to the library to recite. When word got around that the prize for the recitations was to be a night away from home, more joined in and the school was abuzz with children practicing their poems. The second year only the fourth grade was allowed to participate because there had been such an overwhelming response that there was a danger that otherwise so many children might earn the right to the year-end party that there wouldn't be sufficient space.

Children were allowed to catch up on the idea anytime during the school year. In other words, they were allowed to join at any time if they memorized all the poems.

You may be able to get local businesses to sponsor this poetry idea with prizes and food.

Poetry Party

Although children love the idea of a sleep-over, it may be impossible for you to organize because of lack of space, chaperones, or insurance obstacles. If this is the case, you can use another carrot as the prize for memorizing ten poems. Have a poetry party with refreshments and maybe even a poetry-reciting clown or magician.

Poetry Pockets

Each child and adult in your group should choose a poem, original or copied from a book, to keep in his or her poetry pocket. When you meet someone in the hall or at the pencil sharpener, she will say, "Do you have a poem in your pocket?" Your response is to bring out your choice, and read it.

Poetry Pen Pals

Exchange poetry with a poetry pen pal. Children love to get mail, but often don't know what to say when they write to a friend, relative, or assigned pen pal. Suggest that it would be fun to send a poem to share.

Calendar Poetry

Choose a poem for each day of the year and post it as the "poem of the day." Celebrate Poetry Break Day, now listed in *Chase's Calendar of Events* as January 13. This is a good time to inaugurate a poetry break program or start a new year of poetry breaks.

Wear a Poem

Hang a poster printed with a favorite poem around your neck on a string, or pin a poster to your clothes. You become the poetry exhibit. A plastic baggie can hold a poem as well. Wear one so that you'll always have a poem to keep you company.

Dress a Poem

Do you have a cape, apron, appliqued jacket, or hat that you think you would always like to wear as an identifiable logo for your poetry presentations? If so, this idea might work well for you. Whenever you are wearing the chosen item, the patrons in your library or students in your school will say to themselves or to each other, "It's time for poetry break."

Or, consider wearing a costume, occasionally, to present your poetry break. Dress up as Mother Goose, an animal, or a historic figure.

23

Writing Poetry

Your poetry break listeners will be inspired to try writing their own poetry. This is certainly a desirable response to your repeated poetry offerings. You need not direct this initial enthusiasm too strictly, but you might suggest that poetry does have standard forms, and they may want to copy the form of one of their favorite poems. Experimenting with rhythm and words is the best way to begin.

Appreciating Poets

Your listeners may want to find more poetry by a particular poet. The library's poetry collection should yield a wealth of single-author volumes.

Extending the Poetry Break with Literature

You can extend the poetry break into a literature program by reading aloud from a book on a subject related to the poem to create a mini-program. Throughout this anthology, picture books are listed when they team well with a particular poem. Consider presenting the poem, sharing the book, then reading the poem again after you have read the book.

If your own local school or public library does not own the book listed, browse through your library's collection. You are sure to find the perfect book to present to your group. Keep in mind, as well, that the book you share aloud does not have to key to the poem you have chosen for that day. The poetry books you share or simply booktalk are part of your daily literature-sharing time.

PART TWO

USING THE POEMS

5

Act It Out

My friend, frantic, called to tell me her talented daughter had been passed over for the lead in the senior-class musical because she was too tall and would have towered over her leading man. The girl was so disappointed that she was making life miserable for the entire family and was threatening all sorts of "get even" ploys against the production's director. I was sympathetic and offered to take Lisa to tea so that she could vent her frustration on me rather than Mr. Barns. I told Lisa about the time that I auditioned for a college play—not as the lead, but as the housekeeper with three lines—and didn't make it. Much to my delight, though, the director decided to offer some entr'acte entertainment in the form of poetry recitations. Two other disappointed actors and I got to wear costumes and recite poetry during the intermissions. We had the full attention of the audience, and were able to tell our parents that we had performed on stage. Looking over some old photographs and clippings, I was surprised to see that we (not the play) had been featured in the newspaper. Between tears, Lisa just stared as she listened to this story from an old lady, but the next day she suggested to the director that she could do one musical number as an introduction to the whole play. At the first performance, she received a satisfying round of applause even before the curtain opened.

Acting out a poem will give your poetry break volunteers a chance to be dramatic without having to learn the script of a long play or interact with other players, props, and scenery. Use the poetry break as an opportunity to feel like you are in a play without the play.

This technique will also give your group a chance to get up from their seats and help present a poem by illustrating the words with actions, vocal changes, and facial expressions. These poems can be used to vary the poetry break presentations and might also be considered for a more formal presentation to parents or another class. The poems can also be used between acts when putting on a play or as an introduction to a lesson, story, or to add a little movement to an otherwise sedentary day.

As in the other sections in this collection, the poems here may be recited by one person, read aloud, or presented in a chorus. However, these seem particularly suited to individual or group actions.

Begin by reading the poem aloud, perhaps during a poetry break. Subsequently, suggest that the next time the poem is presented, it might be done by the group. The best way for an entire group to memorize a poem is to read it out loud several times. Read it as you would present it. Don't try to slow it down to make it easier to learn. The poem will be memorized more easily if the listeners can hear its rhythm. They will learn it as naturally as they do the words to popular songs.

If the entire group will eventually be performing the same actions in concert, you may want to have two or three children demonstrate the poem to the others with appropriate actions.

The interpretations that follow are, of course, only meant to be suggestions to get you started. Let the children discuss how they might present the poem. You will be surprised to discover who in your group comes up with the best ideas for dramatizing. They may not be the same children who do well in other areas.

In some of these poems children will be miming actions. Mimes study for years until they can make an audience "see" what they are doing. Don't expect your students to be experts, but help them with suggestions. Practice the action with a prop and then repeat the poem, miming the action without a concrete object.

Ideas for staging accompany the poems for easy reference. Some of these may spark your imagination as well as your children's but they will have their own ideas about how to perform each poem.

If you like this idea of acting out a poem, you will want to search for additional poems to act out. Not every poem will lend itself naturally to adding actions. In some cases, it would actually detract from the words to physically act out a poem. Experiment with the poems and with the performers to see which selections work well as theater.

If a particular poem works better when performed by one person and everyone in the group is volunteering to "be in the play, please," suggest that different children go to each classroom with the same poem or that, on subsequent days, others may have their chance to perform the same selection.

Children will feel more comfortable if they make up actions that spring from the text and feel natural to them; if the actions are imposed on them, the children will look and feel rigid and strained. Movement and gesture make it easier to memorize a poem, but may make it more difficult to perform. The inexperienced presenter may be worrying about what to do with her hands instead of concentrating on the words and meaning. So, let the children practice several times, until the actions and words flow easily together.

ACT IT OUT POEMS

Mitten Song • Marie Louise Allen

I Wish I Could Wiggle My Nose • Sharon Burstein

Are You the Guy? • Anonymous

Mouse in Her Room • Anonymous

Lazy Jane • Shel Silverstein

About the Teeth of Sharks • John Ciardi

Imaginary Room • Sylvia Cassedy

How to Assemble a Toy • John Ciardi

Potato Chips • Anthony Gallagher

Buggity • Karla Kuskin

Dragon • Karla Kuskin

Sitting on the Fence • Michael Leunig

Crocodile's Brushing His Teeth • Colin McNaughton

Peter Ping and Patrick Pong • Dennis Lee

Passing Fair • Lillian Morrison

The Mitten Song

by Marie Louise Allen

"Thumbs in the thumb-place,
Fingers all together!"
This is the song
We sing in mitten-weather,
When it is cold,
It doesn't matter whether
Mittens are wool,
Or made of finest leather—
This is the song
We sing in mitten-weather:
"Thumbs in the thumb-place,
Fingers all together!"

This will work well as a leader-response poem. Children join in on the chorus:
"Thumbs in the thumb-place,
Fingers all together!"
As they chant, they hold up first their thumbs and then their hands as though showing that they are wearing mittens.

If you live in a cold climate where the children own mittens, you can have a chorus of mitten-wearers who hold up their bemittened hands at the end of the poem.

For those who live in places like Miami Beach, as I do, consider making over-sized paper or poster-board mittens that can be decorated by children with scenes from their favorite books about snow.

Share:
Brett, Jan. *The Mitten*. Art by the author. Putnam, 1989.
Cauley, Lorinda B. *The Three Little Kittens*. Art by the author. Putnam, 1982.
Rogers, Jean. *Runaway Mittens*. Art by Rie Muñoz. Greenwillow, 1988.

I Wish I Could Wiggle My Nose

by Sharon Burstein

I wish I could wiggle my nose,
As easily as I do toes.
    How did the rabbit
    Master that habit?
I wish I could wiggle my nose.

Your whole group can recite this one as they wiggle their toes and try to wiggle their noses.

Are You the Guy?

Anonymous

Are you the guy
That told the guy
That I'm the guy
That gave the guy
The black eye?

No, I'm not the guy
That told the guy
That you're the guy
That gave the guy
The black eye!

Try reciting this using stylized pugilistic poses. Several presenters, each with a partner, can act this out.

Share:

Carrier, Roch. *The Boxing Champion*. Art by Sheldon Cohen. Tr. from original French by Sheila Fishman. Tundra, 1991.

Mouse in Her Room

Anonymous

A mouse in her room woke Miss Dowd;
She was frightened and screamed very loud,
    Then a happy thought hit her—
    To scare off the critter,
She sat up in bed and meowed.

This is a great choice for a "ham." Announce the poetry break and lie down on the teacher's or librarian's desk. Recite the rhyme. On the last line sit up and "Meow." When this is presented on subsequent occasions the audience will join you with the "Meow."

Lazy Jane

by Shel Silverstein

Lazy
lazy
lazy
lazy
lazy
lazy
Jane,
she
wants
a
drink
of
water
so
she
waits
and
waits
and
waits
and
waits
and
waits
for
it
to
rain.

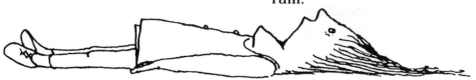

You can use a similar staging for this poem to that for "Mouse in Her Room," reciting it while lying on the desk. After the last line, just open your mouth and wait for a moment.

Share:
Lobel, Arnold. *A Treeful of Pigs*. Art by Anita Lobel. Greenwillow, 1979.
   The farmer is too busy sleeping to help care for the pigs.

About the Teeth of Sharks

by John Ciardi

The thing about a shark is—teeth,
One row above, one row beneath.

Now take a close look. Do you find
It has another row behind?

Still closer—here, I'll hold your hat:
Has it a third behind that?

Now, look in and . . . Look out! Oh my,
I'll never know now! Well, goodbye.

One person portrays the shark and opens his arms in a giant circle representing the open mouth of the shark. The second person can put his or her head in the circle and get "eaten." They can recite together or a third person can concentrate on the recitation while the poem is acted out by the shark and victim.

Share:
Cerullo, Mary M. *Sharks: Challengers of the Deep*. Photos by Jeffrey L. Rotman. Cobblehill, 1993. (Grades 3–5.)

Imaginary Room

by Sylvia Cassedy

To fashion a room—
a room of your own—
fasten your hands
one to the other,
hollow to hollow,
as though
you were holding
a bird—
a swallow, let's say,
or a finch:
something small,
pinched,
and pressed
in the well
of your palms
like an almond
at rest
in its shell.

    The presenter can cup her hands at the end of the poem to show the imaginary room.

Share:
Bare, Colleen Stanley. *This is a House.* Photos by author. Dutton, 1992.
Dorros, Arthur. *This is My House.* Art by the author. Scholastic, 1992.
Hoberman, Mary Ann. *A House is a House for Me.* Art by Betty Fraser. Viking, 1978.

How to Assemble a Toy

by John Ciardi

This is the whatsit that fits on the knob
Of the gadget that turns the thingamabob.
This is the dingus that fits in place
With the doodad next to the whosiface.
This is the jigger that goes in the hole
Where the gizmo turns the rigamarole.
Now slip the ding-dang into the slot
of the jugamalug, and what have you got?

It's a genuine neverwas such a not!

Two or many more can enjoy this one. Recite the poem first; on subsequent readings children, young adults, or adults can pretend to be gizmos, rigamorales, and ding-dangs.

Share:
Williams, Karen Lynn. *Galimoto*. Art by Catherine Stock. Lothrop, 1990.
    Kondi is determined to search through the village to find the materials and make a toy.

Potato Chips

by Anthony E. Gallagher

A potato chip is something
Never ceasing to amuse.
I love its funny wrinkles
And the crunchy way it chews.

After you have used this poem a number of times, let the group recite it. On the last line pull out bags of potato chips and crunch off the stage. Potato chips make an easy to serve snack and souvenir. Hand out chips to the audience and everyone can join in a finale of crunching.

Buggity

by Karla Kuskin

Buggity
Buggity
Bug
Wandering aimlessly
Buggishly smug
When all of a sudden along came a shoe
Out with another shoe
Wandering too.
The shoes went on wandering:
Left,
Right,
Left,
Splat.

Bugs
Very frequently perish like that.

    As you present this, take off your shoes and "walk" them with your hands on the desk or table top, pretending to crush a bug when the poem cues you. (Remember to wear easily removeable shoes when you plan to present this.) Your group can recite and act out "Buggity" together. Just make sure that you have enough time to put your shoes back on and get on with the day.

Share:
Facklam, Margery. *The Big Bug Book.* Art by Paul Facklam. Little, 1994.
    Big bugs are described and are illustrated in their actual sizes—BIG.
Parker, Nancy Winslow, and Joan Richards Wright. *Bugs.* Art by Nancy Winslow Parker.
    Greenwillow, 1987.

Dragon

by Karla Kuskin

Let me tell you about me.
Children love me,
You're a child.
All my heads are green and handsome.
All my eyes are red and wild.
All my toes have claws upon them.
All the claws have hooks.
I blow smoke through all my noses.
It is hotter than it looks.
All my tails have points upon them.
All my teeth are sharp and blue.
I won't bite you very badly.
I am fond of you.
All my scales are shaped like arrows.
They will hurt you if you touch.
So, although I know you love me,
Do not pet me very much.

On the last line of the poem children can show their blue teeth. Make them out of construction paper.

Share:

Prelutsky, Jack. *The Dragons Are Singing Tonight.* Art by Peter Sis.

Contemporary poems about dragons with art to share.

Sitting on the Fence

by Michael Leunig

'Come sit down beside me',
I said to myself,
And although it doesn't make sense,
I held my own hand
As a small sign of trust
And together I sat on the fence.

Two or three presenters can sit on a desk or table representing the fence. On the last line they can hold hands. Mix boys and girls together so that the audience can react to Kim holding hands with Carlos.

The Crocodile's Brushing His Teeth

by Colin McNaughton

The crocodile's brushing his teeth, I'm afraid,
This certainly means we're too late.
The crocodile's brushing his teeth, I'm afraid,
He has definitely put on some weight.
The crocodile's brushing his teeth, I'm afraid.
It really is, oh, such a bore.
The crocodile's brushing his teeth, I'm afraid,
He appears to have eaten grade four.

A sheet can be the body of the crocodile. On the last line the sheet is removed revealing grade four hiding underneath. Be prepared to recite this poem several times because every one will want their turn to be either the crocodile or one of the members of grade four.

Share:
Waber, Bernard. *Lyle, Lyle, Crocodile.* Art by the author. Houghton, 1965.

Peter Ping and Patrick Pong

by Dennis Lee

When Peter Ping met Patrick Pong
They stared like anything.
For Ping (in fact) looked more like Pong
While Pong looked more like Ping.

The reason was, a nurse had changed
Their cribs, and got them wrong—
So no one knew, their whole lives through,
That Pong was Ping; Ping, Pong.

    Try this with two presenters each reciting a verse and wearing the same hats and big bow ties.

Share:

Greenburg, Dan. *Jumbo the Boy and Arnold the Elephant*. Art by Susan Perl. Harper, 1989.

    Switched at birth, a boy and an elephant bemuse their parents—and readers.

Passing Fair

by Lillian Morrison

There is nothing more fair
than to pluck a long forward pass from the air
on a field of grass . . . except perhaps
to have thrown the pass.

    Act this out in slow motion.

Rice Pudding

by A. A. Milne

What is the matter with Mary Jane?
She's crying with all her might and main,
And she won't eat her dinner—rice pudding again—
What *is* the matter with Mary Jane?

What is the matter with Mary Jane?
I've promised her dolls and a daisy-chain,
And a book about animals—all in vain—
What *is* the matter with Mary Jane?

What is the matter with Mary Jane?
She's perfectly well, and she hasn't a pain;
But, look at her, now she's beginning again!—
What *is* the matter with Mary Jane?

What is the matter with Mary Jane?
I've promised her sweets and a ride in the train,
And I've begged her to stop for a bit and explain—
What *is* the matter with Mary Jane?

What is the matter with Mary Jane?
She's perfectly well and hasn't a pain,
And it's lovely rice pudding for dinner again!—
What *is* the matter with Mary Jane?

Two children might want to act this out, alternating stanzas, with one child reciting a verse while miming offerings to cajole the toddler, and the other student miming Mary Jane's pouts and tantrum.

A Tale Told Standing

by Grace Tall

This is a summer story,
(I'll stand if you don't mind),
And if it has a moral,
It's this: Don't be too kind.
It happened only lately,
And the tale involves a bee
And someone who befriended him
Who happens to be me.
I was walking by the birdbath
When, looking in, I found
Immersed in shallow water
A bumblebee half-drowned.
With the best of good intention
I did what you'd have done—
I placed his little body
On a dry spot in the sun.
Well-pleased to do this kindness
I turned to walk to town,
And that's when it happened.
No, thanks, I won't sit down.

Act out the poem's story, or encourage children to make the sound of the buzzing bees as a background or chorus to the poem.

Share:

Polacco, Patricia. *The Bee Tree*. Art by author. Philomel, 1993.

All ages can follow the bee to its honey tree and a little girl to the joys of reading.

Sheep

by Mike Thaler

When sheep
Can't sleep
Do they make a big fuss,
Or do they just go ahead
And begin
To count
Us?

After one person recites the poem, children walk by the imaginary sleeping sheep and count off. If there are children in the group who speak other languages they can count in their language.

Share:

Hooks, William, and Barbara Brenner. *Lion and the Lamb.* Art by Bruce Degen. Bantam, 1989.

> This early-reading book features a lamb engrossed in a book and a lion who wants to scare her.

Sanders, Scott Russell. *Warm as Wool.* Art by Helen Cogancherry. Bradbury, 1992.

Shaw, Nancy. *Sheep in a Jeep.* Art by Margot Apple. Houghton, 1986.

> First in this author's series of short rhymed text stories with wonderful sheep drawings.

_____. *Sheep Out to Eat.* Art by Margot Apple. Houghton, 1992.

New Kid

by Mike Makley

Our baseball team never did very much,
we had me and PeeWee and Earl and Dutch.
And the Oak Street Tigers always got beat
Until the new kid moved in on our street.

The kid moved in with a mitt and a bat
and an official New York Yankee hat.
The new kid plays shortstop on second base
and can outrun us all in any place.

The kid never muffs a grounder or fly
no matter how hard it's hit or how high.
And the new kid always acts quite polite,
never yelling or spitting or starting a fight.

We were playing the league champs just last week;
they were trying to break our winning streak.
In the last inning the score was one—one,
when the new kid swung and hit a home run.

A few of the kids and their parents say
they don't believe that the new kid should play.
But she's good as me, Dutch, PeeWee, or Earl,
so we don't care that the new kid's a girl.

At the end of the poem, a girl dressed in a baseball outfit can stroll across the room with a ball and glove.

I Had a Little Secret

by Jack Prelutsky

I had a little secret
that I could not wait to tell,
I whispered it to Willa,
who repeated it to Nell.

Nell had to tell Belinda,
who told Laura and Lenore,
I think my little secret
is no secret anymore.

Six girls stand in a row and whisper to each other. Remind the girls that they can't really whisper, but must "stage whisper" the poem, or they will not be heard.

Hands

by Bobbi Katz

Clapping
slapping
finger-snapping
folding
holding
modeling
molding
writing
fighting
stroking
poking
itching
stitching
shaking
taking
squeezing
teasing
pleasing
HANDS!

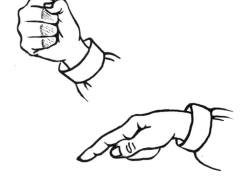

Discuss with the group ways that hands can act out this poem. Kneel behind a table or hold up a piece of black fabric so that only hands will show when presenting this poem with the appropriate gestures.

Company

by Bobbi Katz

I'm fixing a lunch for a dinosaur.
Who knows when one might come by?
I'm pulling up all the weeds I can find,
I'm piling them high as the sky.
I'm fixing a lunch for a dinosaur.
I hope he will stop by soon.
Maybe he'll just walk down my street
And have some lunch at noon.

I'm baking a cake for a garter snake
With sand and a bucket of glop.
You never know when a garter snake
Might wiggle up and stop.
I'm baking a cake for a garter snake
It's best to be prepared—
Because when I see a garter snake
I'm always a little bit scared.

One or two people can recite this poem. Behind them several children can mime the action.

49

An Itch

by Larry Kirkman

One day
    I itched
        on my back
    I couldn't reach it
    I couldn't itch it
        But my friend
            loved to scratch
And he wrote his name
On my back
With his fingernails

This will give your audience a good laugh if you have several friends lined up, facing one direction, and scratching one another's backs.

Great Pitches

by J. Patrick Lewis

The fastball
    that you hope to poke
    is smoke

The curveball
    that you thought was there
    is air

The knuckler
    wobbling up to you
    can dipsy-do

The sinker
    comes as some surprise
    it dies

The let-up pitch
    who can resist?
    you missed

The spitball
    that by law's forbidden
    (is hidden)

Six pitchers—or just one—can mime the action while this poem is recited. You may have to do a bit of research on these pitches if you are not familiar with the terms.

Share:
Blackstone, Margaret. *This Is Baseball.* Art by John O'Brien. Holt, 1993.
    All ages. The essence of the game is described while showing a game in progress.

Cohen, Ron. *My Dad's Baseball*. Art by author. Lothrop, 1994.

> Dad tells about his first ball game.

Mochizuki, Ken. *Baseball Saved Us*. Art by Dom Lee. Lee and Low, 1993.

> A Japanese-American boy learns to play baseball in an internment camp during World War II.

Take Me Out to the Ballgame. Lyrics by Jack Norwood. Art by Alec Gilman. Four Winds, 1993.

Take Me Out to the Ballgame. Lyrics by Jack Norwood. Art by Maryann Kovalski. Scholastic. 1992.

> Compare the cartoon-like drawings of Kovalski and the authentic 1947 setting of the art of Gilman that accompany the words to this long-popular song in these two picture-book versions.

Holding Hands

by Lenore M. Link

Elephants walking
Along the trails

Are holding hands
By holding tails

Trunks and tails
Are handy things

When elephants walk
In circus rings.

Elephants work
And elephants play

And elephants walk
And feel so gay.

And when they walk—
It never fails

They're holding hands
By holding tails.

Your whole group can be involved with this one. Hold hands all around the room. This poem, paired with Bobbi Katz's "Hands" on page 48 would also make a nice pair of partner poems (see chapter 8).

The Wizard Said:

by Richard Edwards

"You find a sheltered spot that faces south . . ."
  "And then?"
"You sniff and put two fingers in your
        mouth . . ."
  "And then?"
"You close your eyes and roll your eyeballs
        round . . ."
  "And then?"
"You lift your left foot slowly off the
        ground . . ."
  "And then?"
"You make your palm into a kind of cup . . ."
  "And then?"
"You *very quickly* raise your right foot up . . ."
  "And then?"
"You fall over."

Have two people dramatize this, or let the whole group attempt to follow the directions. Make sure everyone has a lot of space to fall over at the end. And be prepared for some silly behavior.

6

Art Activities

In Indiana, I was presented with a booklet of drawings illustrating the poems that I collected for my *Windy Day* anthology (HarperCollins, 1988). A fourth-grade class had read the book and each child had chosen one poem to re-illustrate. The result is a lovely book to cherish, but also a sample of an excellent way to expand the poetry break into art activities.

You don't have to be an artist yourself to lead art activities. Your group may want to respond to poems they hear with a picture, a poster, a banner, or the creation of an artifact. This can happen with any poem used in the poetry break, but the poems in this chapter have been selected because they have proved particularly successful when connected to art activities.

The students' art in the poetry collection I received was beautiful. In general, art education in the United States is undervalued and we need to encourage our students to form the "art habit." We would like them to think visually and also to feel more comfortable about drawing, painting, and sculpting. Expressing their feelings about poetry through art may be a start to a lifelong interest in visual arts.

It is important to have art supplies ready and waiting when the creative spirit moves, or when you, as leader, decide that it's time to give the children an opportunity to respond artistically. The projects suggested are just intended to give you a few ideas to help you and your children get started.

Share these books any time you use art with poetry:
Dodds, Dayle Ann. *The Color Box.* Art by Giles Laroche. Little, Brown, 1992.

A monkey explores a box filled with color.
Isaacson, Philip M. *A Short Walk Around the Pyramids and Through the World of Art.* Illustrated with photographs. Knopf, 1993. (Grades 3–6.)

This attractive chapter book is a survey of architecture and art. Too long to share in one sitting, it can be enjoyed a chapter at a time.

McMillan, Bruce. *Growing Colors*. Photos by the author. Lothrop, 1988.

    Clear, vibrant photographs show the color in the food we eat.

Rosen, Michael. *How the Animals Got Their Colors*. Art by John Clementson. Harcourt, 1992.

    Share one or all nine of these tales about animals and the origins of their colors.

ART ACTIVITIES POEMS

Wheels, Wheels, Wheels

by Nancy White Carlstrom

Big cars, brown cars
Rolling through the town cars

Big trucks, white trucks
Rolling through the night trucks

Big trains, black trains
Rolling on the track trains

Car wheels, truck wheels
Wheels on trains

Rolling in the sunshine
Rolling in the rain

Round and round
Fast and slow

Wheels are rolling
There they go

Rolling along
Singing a song

Zoom brr-room
Zoom brr-room

Wheels, wheels, wheels.

Draw or construct as many vehicles you can think of and include a variety of wheels to keep them running. This makes an impressive mural. Make the wheels moveable by using brads available in the stationery department. Consider trying this with children of varying ages.

Share:

Carlstrom, Nancy White. *Wheels, Wheels, Wheels.* Art by Roni Shepherd.
  Big Book from Scott, Foresman, 1993.

Aerobics

by Richard Edwards

Bend and stretch,
Stretch and bend,
Bend and stretch all day;
Squat down small,
Jump up tall,
What a game to play!
Though I'm young and beautiful,
I feel old and grey,
I'm sure it isn't natural
To exercise this way.

One and two,
Two and one,
One and two and three;
Up and down
Like a clown,
Oh, my aching knee!
If you want an easy life,
Take a tip from me:
A princess in a pop-up book
Is not the thing to be.

To make the simplest type of pop-up to use when you share this poem, fold a piece of posterboard to look like a book. Draw your version of the princess. Cut her out and affix the bottom of the cutout to the center of a sheet of paper that you also fold in half. Paste one side of that paper to each inner side of your posterboard "book," folding the princess down along the middle, so that she pops up when the book is opened. Explore Joan Irvine's book listed below for more complex techniques.

Share:

Andersen, Hans Christian. *The Princess and the Pea.* Art by Dorothee Duntze. North-South, 1985.

Johnston, Tony. *The Cowboy and the Black-Eyed Pea.* Art by Warren Ludwig. Putnam, 1992.

Irvine, Joan. *How to Make Super Pop-Ups.* Art by Linda Hendry. Morrow, 1992.

Pencil and Paint

by Eleanor Farjeon

Winter has a pencil
For pictures clear and neat,
She traces the black treetops
Upon a snowy sheet,
But autumn has a palette
And a painting brush instead,
And daubs the leaves for pleasure
With yellow, brown, and red.

Use pencil and paints to recreate the contrasting images inspired by this poem.

The Zebra's Photo

Chris Hogan

I snapped it in colour
. . . This photo's not right!
Just look at this zebra!
. . . It's in black and white!

To present this poem, draw a simple camera on one side of a piece of paper. On the other side, draw a picture of a black and white zebra. When reciting the poem hold the camera side up and on the last line turn the picture over to show the zebra.

Paper Boat

by Gerda Mayer

Make a little paper boat,
Take it to the river,
If it swims and stays afloat,
You will live forever.

Create a boat from paper. Does your boat float? Try it in a sink, bathtub, or lake.

Share:
Kleven, Elisa. *The Paper Princess*. Art by the author. Dutton, 1994.
Small, David. *Paper John*. Art by the author. Farrar, 1987.

John folds paper boats for the children in town, but one day the Devil comes to town.

Gold-Tinted Dragon

by Karla Kuskin

What's the good of a wagon
Without any dragon
To pull you for mile after mile?
An elegant lean one
A gold-tinted green one
Wearing a dragonly smile.
You'll sweep down the valleys,
You'll sail up the hills
Your dragon will shine in the sun
And as you rush by
The people will cry
"I wish that my wagon had one!"

Design your own dragon in collage or paint.

Share:

Enderle, Judith Ross, and Stephanie Gordon Tessler. *The Good-for-Something Dragon.*
Art by Les Gray. Boyds Mill, 1993.

John wants to keep the baby dragon Ashley but must find a "use" for her to please
his father, Sir Simon.

Sis, Peter. *Komodo.* Art by the author. Greenwillow, 1993.

A young boy and his family visit an island in Indonesia to find a real dragon.

Mural on Second Avenue

by Lilian Moore

Someone
stood here
tall on a ladder,
dreaming
to the slap of a
wet brush,

painting
on the blank
unwindowed wall of
this old house.

Now the wall is a
field of wild
grass,
bending to a wind.

A unicorn's grazing there
beside a
zebra.

A giraffe
is nibbling a
treetop

and in a sky of
eye-blinking
blue

a horse is flying.

63

All
right at home in the
neighborhood.

Create your own class mural on paper or . . . will someone lend you a wall?
When your mural is complete, make up a poem to celebrate it.

Purple

by Jeff Moss

If purple was the only color in the world
You would read about "Snow Purple and The Seven Dwarfs."
You would sing about
   "The Purple Grass Growing All Around, All Around,"
And you would drink purple juice for breakfast.
You'd write with chalk on the purpleboard,
And cross the street when the light turned purple,
And visit the President of the United States in the Purple House.
You could even write a poem that begins:

   Roses are purple, violets are purple . . .

It's a good thing there are other colors.

   Draw a purple world.

What is Orange?

by Mary O'Neil

Orange is a tiger lily,
A carrot,
A feather from
A parrot,
A flame,
The wildest color
You can name.
Orange is a happy day
Saying good-by
In a sunset that
Shocks the sky.
Orange is brave
Orange is bold
It's bittersweet
And marigold.
Orange is zip
Orange is dash
The brightest stripe
In a Roman sash.
Orange is an orange
Also a mango
Orange is music
Of the tango.
Orange is the fur
Of the fiery fox,
The brightest crayon
In the box.
And in the fall
When the leaves are turning
Orange is the smell
Of a bonfire burning.

Create an art masterpiece using only your favorite color to fashion your own-colored world. Is it still your favorite?

Share:

Bragg, Ruth Gambicki. *Colors of the Day*. Art by the author. Picture Book Studio, 1992.
Rossetti, Christina. *Color*. Art by Mary Teichman. Harper, 1992.
    Colorful art for Rossetti's poem.
Westray, Kathleen. *A Color Sampler*. Art by the author. Ticknor and Fields, 1993.
    Examines colors and how to mix them.

The Inventor Thinks Up Helicopters

by Patricia Hubbell

"Why not
a
vertical
whirling
winding
bug,
that hops like a cricket
crossing a rug,
that swerves like a dragonfly
testing his steering,
twisting and veering?
Fleet as a beetle.
Up
down
left
right,
jounce, bounce, day and night.
It could land in a pasture the size of a dot . . .
Why not?"

Draw a new invention—something so wonderful that poets will write about it.

7

Choral Reading

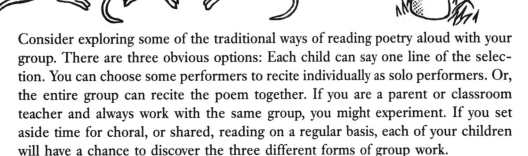

Consider exploring some of the traditional ways of reading poetry aloud with your group. There are three obvious options: Each child can say one line of the selection. You can choose some performers to recite individually as solo performers. Or, the entire group can recite the poem together. If you are a parent or classroom teacher and always work with the same group, you might experiment. If you set aside time for choral, or shared, reading on a regular basis, each of your children will have a chance to discover the three different forms of group work.

Reciting the whole poem together is the easiest and quickest technique. Each child should have a copy of the poem. If everyone can see the chalkboard easily, the text can be displayed there. This will save you time and the rattle of papers. (It may even save you from being hit on the head with a paper airplane after the session.)

As leader, you will want to begin by reciting with the group so that they know at what pace to proceed and can follow your signals for reading in unison. The group tendency is to recite sluggishly without enthusiasm, since each individual is playing it safe by following the lead of the person next to him or her. When you feel that you have mastered group work, you can experiment with the other forms of choral reading.

Try to give each child in your group a chance to "be the star." We have a tendency to choose the child who has already proved herself when it comes to presenting orally. If your superindendent is visiting with a delegation of foreign educators and you want to impress them—or at least not appear incompetent—you would be foolish not to show off your best pupils. When it is just your own class or school, why not give everyone a chance to excel?

Try some of the poems in this section to see if you enjoy implementing the choral-recitation concept. If you do, you are sure to discover other poems in this book and other collections that your group will want to perform.

CHORAL READING POEMS

A Peanut Sat on a Railroad Track • Anonymous

Somersaults and Headstands • Kathleen Fraser

The Zoo • Frank Asch

Conversation • Eve Merriam

There's Music in a Hammer • Anonymous

Ice Cream • Rick Kilcup

The Answers • Robert Clairmont

Coyotes • Jon Whyte

Coincidence • Claudia Lewis

Thoughts on Talkers • Walter R. Brooks

Jelly Beans • Aileen Fisher

A Boy and His Dog • Zaro Weil

Haircut • Yoshiko Uchida

Jenny the Juvenile Juggler • Dennis Lee

Harry the Hawk • Margaret Mahy

Fishes' Evening Song • Dahlov Ipcar

Beans, Beans, Beans • Jones L. Hymes and Lucia Hymes

A Peanut Sat On a Railroad Track

Anonymous

A peanut sat on a railroad track,
His heart was all a-flutter;
The five-fifteen came rushing by—
Toot! Toot! Peanut butter!

Divide the group into two separate groups. Tell Group A that they will say "Toot! Toot!" and Group B that they will say "Peanut butter!" This poem is short and you will want to recite the whole poem once together. On the next recitation, let the two groups chime in. If time allows, do it yet again, as the students will now have confidence and timing.

When you next try this poem, the listeners may want to use hand motions to show the size of the peanut, the train whistle being pulled, and by rubbing their palms together, indicate the peanut butter.

Somersaults and Headstands

by Kathleen Fraser

What are you doing?
     I'm turning a somersault.
How do you do it?
     I put my head on the grass
     and roll over like a snail.
Could you turn a wintersault?
     No, because my head would
     get cold in the snow.

Now, what are you doing?
     A headstand.
Is it like a somersault?
     Well, sort of, but you stop
     in the middle.
How do you keep from falling?
     I pretend everyone else
     is walking upside down.

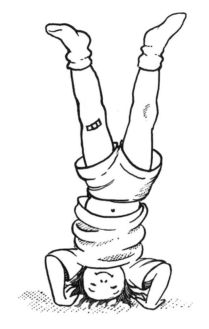

This works best as a two-person recitation with one voice the questioner, the other the acrobat.

The Zoo

by Frank Asch

Everyone tries
To get the lions
       to roar
But they roar
When they want to
And not before.

Divide the children into two groups. Group A recites the first three lines, Group B recites the last three. The second time that you recite this, choose five or six listeners to be the lions and have them roar at the end of the poem.

Conversation

by Eve Merriam

"Buenas días," says Señor Rías.
"Bonjour," says Monsieur Dutour.
"Buon giorno," says Signor Tiorno.
"Hello," says Mister Coe.

"Buenas noches," says Señora Rochas.
"Bonne nuit," says Madame La Brie.
"Buona notte," says Signora Capolotte.
"Good night," says Mrs. White.

"Hasta luego," says Señorita Diego.
"Au revoir," says Mademoiselle Loire.
"Arrivederci," says Signorina Terci.
"See you soon," says Miss Calhoun.

This poem can be performed with four people reading the parts mentioned, each person saying one line, or the four players can read only the conversation and a narrator can say the rest.

Rehearse the proper pronunciations of the foreign phrases and the names before the children read the poem aloud. They will soon be saying "hello" in four languages.

There's Music in a Hammer

Anonymous

There's music in a hammer
There's music in a nail.
There's music in a pussy cat,
When you step upon her tail.

This short, silly rhyme can be recited with gusto by an entire group. At the end of the poem, add some spirited cat wails.

Ice Cream

by Rick Kilcup

Ice cream, ice cream!
Attack it with a spoon!
Oh golly, darn, phooey, rats . . .
It's always gone too soon!

Try this as a round. Start the second group after the first line. Use a little syncopation for lively effect.

The Answers

by Robert Clairmont

"When did the world begin and how?"
I asked a lamb, a goat, a cow:

"What's it all about and why?"
I asked a hog as he went by:

"Where will the whole thing end, and when?"
I asked a duck, a goose, a hen:

And I copied all the answers too,
A quack, a honk, an oink, a moo.

Divide the class into two groups. The first group asks the question, the second answers. When they reach the last line, the groups can recite alternate words. Add appropriate animal sounds on your next reading.

Coyotes

by Jon Whyte

The coyotes are howling;
  it's forty below.
The moon is silvering
  shivering snow.

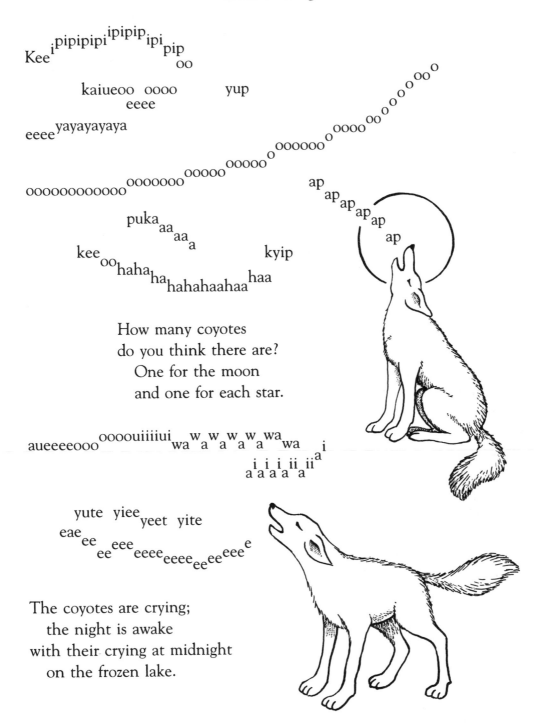

Keeⁱpipipipi^{ipipip}ipi_{pip}
_{oo}

kaiueoo oooo   yup
_{eeee}

eeee^{yayayayaya}

oooooooooooo^{ooooooo}ooooo^{ooooo}o^{oooooo}o^{oooo}oo^{oooo}oo^ooo^o

ap
ap_{ap}_{ap}_{ap}
ap

puka_{aa}_{aa}_a

kee_{oo}haha_{ha}_{hahahaahaa}haa   kyip

How many coyotes
do you think there are?
One for the moon
and one for each star.

aueeeeooo^{oooouiiiiui}wa^wa^wa^wa^wa^{wa}wa   i
i i i ii ii^a
a^aa^aa

yute yiee_{yeet yite}
eae_{ee}
ee^{eee}eeee_{eeee}_{ee}ee^{eee}^e

The coyotes are crying;
  the night is awake
with their crying at midnight
  on the frozen lake.

This is a good selection for days when your group is restless, i.e., "being impossible." Let them howl like coyotes at a given signal for the appropriate sound effects as you recite this poem. Start them out by trying the transliterated sounds the poet has provided. On later renditions, they may take a bit of "poetic license" in customizing their howls.

Share:

Aardema, Vera. *Borrequita and the Coyote.* Art by Petra Mathers. Knopf, 1991.

Lund, Jillian. *Way Out West Lives a Coyote Named Frank.* Art by the author. Dutton, 1993.

Taylor, Harriet Peck. *Coyote Places the Stars.* Art by the author. Bradbury, 1993.

Coincidence

by Claudia Lewis

My mother's best friend
from around the block
would pop in the door
without ringing
or knocking
but always called out
"Hoo Hoo!"

One day, bringing a pie,
she called
"Hoo Hoo!"
just as the bird in our clock
sprang out and sang
"Cuckoo!"

We never forgot!

Three people can help present this poem. Use a narrator, mother's best friend, and the bird who cries, "Cuckoo."

Thoughts on Talkers

by Walter R. Brooks

Some people talk in a telephone
And some people talk in a hall;
Some people talk in a whisper,
And some people talk in a drawl;
And some people talk-and-talk-and-talk-and-talk-and-talk
And never say anything at all.

Five people can each recite one line, then they can all read the last line together. Try using a variety of voices with this or even think about using costumes and props to give each character a distinctive personality.

Jelly Beans

by Aileen Fisher

"I like white ones."
   "Here are two."
"I like blacks."
   "But there are so few."
"I want pink ones."
   "Two for you."
"I like orange."
   "What shall we do—
   there isn't an orange,
   I've looked them through."
"Awwww."
   "Wait! here's a red,
   and a yellow too—
   That'll make orange
   when you get through."

Two voices or two groups can share the dialogue in this rhyme. And think about giving everyone jelly beans as a souvenir/treat.

A Boy and His Dog

by Zaro Weil

Boy: Here dog
Dog: Woof
Boy: Good dog
Dog: Woof woof
Boy: Now sit
Dog: Woof woof woof
Boy: Now stand
Dog: Woof woof woof woof
Boy: Roll over
Dog: Woof woof woof woof woof
Boy: Now speak
Dog: Here boy

The poet has nicely scripted this poem so that it is ready to present with two voices: Boy and Dog. Prediction: Everyone will want to play the dog.

Haircut

by Yoshiko Uchida

Snip, snip . . .
    Not too short!
Snip, snip . . .
    Not too short!
Snip, snip . . .
    Ohh, TOO SHORT!
Don't worry,
It will grow!

The barber and his or her client recite this as a two-voice poem that they'll want to act out, too.

Share:

Mitchell, Margaree King. *Uncle Jed's Barbershop.* Art by James Ransome. Simon and Schuster, 1993.

> After years of saving and sacrifice, Uncle Jed realizes his dream of having his own barbershop.

Jenny the Juvenile Juggler

by Dennis Lee

Jenny had hoops she could sling in the air
And she brought them along to the Summerhill Fair.
And a man from a carnival sideshow was there,
Who declared that he needed a juggler.

And it's
   Oops! Jenny, whoops! Jenny,
   Swing along your hoops, Jenny,
   Spin a little pattern as you go;
Because it's
   Oops! Jenny's hoops! Jenny,
   Sling a loop-the-loop, Jenny,
   Whoops! Jenny, oops! Jenny, O!

Well, the man was astonished at how the hoops flew,
And he said, "It's amazing what some kids can do!"
And now at the carnival, Act Number Two
Is Jenny the Juvenile Juggler.

And it's
 Oops! Jenny, whoops! Jenny,
 Swing along your hoops, Jenny,
 Spin a little pattern as you go;
Because it's
 Oops! Jenny's hoops, Jenny.
 Sling a loop-the-loop, Jenny,
 Whoops! Jenny, oops! Jenny, O!

This works well with a narrator and a chorus for the "Oops! Jenny, whoops! Jenny."

Harry the Hawk

by Margaret Mahy

Harry the Hawk on his magic trapeze
Flies over the roofs of the city with ease.
He hangs by his heels and he swings by his knees.
Tumultuous Harry the Hawk.

He has the grand acrobatical style.
Stop when you see him and watch for a while.
He has a secret tucked into his smile.
Mysterious Harry the Hawk.

If he should fall there's no need for dismay,
He'll just give a laugh that is gallant and gay.
Spreading his wings, he'll go floating away.
That's why he's Harry the Hawk.

Bird boy with never a fret or a care,
Woven of sunshine and warm summer air,
Sparrows and stars in the net of his hair.
FANTASTICAL Harry the Hawk.

The last line of each verse can be echoed by the group. For a class circus mini-theme, pair this with the previous poem, "Jenny the Juvenile Juggler" by Dennis Lee.

Fishes' Evening Song

by Dahlov Ipcar

Flip flop,
Flip flap,
Slip slap,
Lip lap;
Water sounds,
Soothing sounds.
We fan our fins
As we lie
Resting here
Eye to eye.
Water falls
Drop by drop,
Plip plop,
Plink plunk,
Splish splash;
Fish fins fan,
Fish tails swish,
Swush, swash, swish.
This we wish . . .
Water cold,
Water clear,
Water smooth,
Just to soothe
Sleepy fish.

Two groups echoing each other in alternate lines will give listeners the hypnotic rhythm of swimming fish.

Beans, Beans, Beans

by Jones L. Hymes and Lucia Hymes

Baked beans,
Butter beans,
Big, fat lima beans,
Long, thin string beans—
These are just a few.

Green beans,
Black beans,
Big, fat kidney beans,
Red hot chili beans,
Jumping beans, too.

Pea beans,
Pinto beans,
Don't forget shelly beans,
Last of all, best of all,
I like jelly beans.

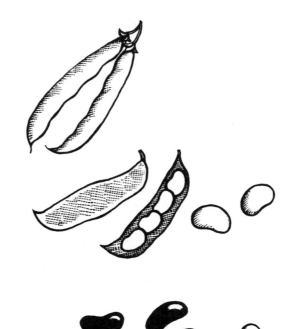

This makes a good chant with different groups calling out the items on this list.

Share:

Butterworth, Nick, and Mick Inkpen. *Jasper's Beanstalk.* Bradbury, 1993.

A cat plants a bean and . . . eventually it sprouts. Simple drawings and a short text.

8

Making "Music"

When the English language is arranged as poetry, many people consider it a form of music. This is one of the reasons that it is often suggested that poetry be read aloud for the fullest enjoyment. Playing music while you listen to poems may be one way to present poetry in a memorable fashion. Allow your students to help you choose the proper music to accompany favorite poems.

Children might also enjoy the idea of making their own music—or noise—to play while reciting a poem. And lucky you, if you can sing. Song lyrics are a form of poetry, too. Sing your poetry break!

You might share any of these books whenever you feature music in your poetry break:

Fleischman, Paul. *Rondo in C.* Art by Janet Wentworth. Harper, 1988.

What do you think about when music is played?

Griffith, Helen V. *Georgia Music.* Art by James Stevenson. Greenwillow, 1986.

A little girl brings Georgia music to her Grandfather.

Monceaux, Morgan. *Jazz: My Music. My People.* Art by the author. Knopf, 1994.

Ober, Hal. *How Music Came to the World.* Art by Carol Ober. Houghton, 1994.

Page, P.K. *The Travelling Musicians of Bremen.* Art by Kady MacDonald Denton. Little, 1991.

Four animal friends surprise a den of thieves with their music.

Rayner, Mary. *Garth Pig Steals the Show.* Art by author. Dutton, 1993.

Who is the mysterious sousaphone player in the Pig family band?

MAKING MUSIC POEMS

Sorting Out the Kitchen Pans • Quentin Blake

A Band of Gorrillas • Patricia Hooper

Song of the Pop-Bottlers • Morris Bishop

Alarm Clock • Eve Merriam

Whistle • Anonymous

The Girl Who Makes the Cymbals Bang • X. J. Kennedy

Here Comes the Band • William Cole

Roadside Peddlers • Monica Gunning

Sorting Out the Kitchen Pans

by Quentin Blake

We're sorting out the Kitchen Pans
    DING   DONG   BANG
Sorting out the Kitchen Pans
    BING   BONG   CLANG

Sorting out the Kitchen Pans
    TING   BANG   DONG
Sorting out the Kitchen Pans
    CLANG   DING   BONG

Collect pots and pans and bring along a spoon or two and you have ready-made instruments to use with this poem. Children's voices can shout out the chorus of DING DONG BANG and BING BONG CLANG. Other children can bang their pots, hopefully in a controlled, rhythmic fashion. This one might be best for poetry breaks during after-school activities, when other classes won't be disturbed.

Share:
Rockwell, Anne. *Pots and Pans*. Art by Lizzie Rockwell. Macmillan, 1993.

An identification book for preschoolers and primary-age children. Share this with your older children, too, as an example of simplicity with a message.

A Band of Gorillas

by Patricia Hooper

A band of gorillas is coming to town.
They dangle from treetops and drum upside down.
They clang with their cymbals and strum with their feet,
But you'd better watch out if they come down your street!

They tune up their trumpets and toot out their tunes.
They blow on their bugles and blare their bassoons.
But if you look friendly, they'll march through your door,
Straight over your sofa, and camp on the floor!

They'll pound your piano and tweedle their flutes,
They'll twang on your fiddle and stomp with their boots.
They're loud as hyenas and wild as chincillas—
Don't ever make friends with a band of gorillas!

Here is a delightful poem for your whole group to chant and act out. Some of the "gorillas" can play invisible instruments, others can dance to this rhythmic poem.

Song of the Pop-Bottlers

by Morris Bishop

Pop bottles pop–bottles
    In pop shops;
The pop–bottles Pop bottles
    Poor Pop drops.

When Pop drops pop–bottles,
    Pop–bottles plop!
Pop–bottles topple!
    Pop mops slop!

Stop! Pop'll drop bottle,
    Stop, Pop, stop!
When Pop bottles pop–bottles,
    Pop–bottles pop!

You're on your own with this catchy tongue-twister with a story. How about letting the audience chant, quietly and rhythmically, "Pop-bottle, pop-bottle" in the background as one presenter recites the poem. Go through the poem once, so everyone can hear and understand the story, before adding the chant.

Alarm Clock

by Eve Merriam

in the deep sleep forest
there were ferns
there were feathers
there was fur
and a soft ripe peach
on a branch within my
    r-r-r-r-r-r-r-r-r-r-r-r-r-r-r-r-r-r

    Use an alarm clock to end the quiet of this poem, setting it off just after 'r-r-r'.
If you don't want to use clocks, use a chorus of voices imitating their un-favorite
alarm clock, all variations on the 'r-r-r-' sound to maintain the play of words.

Whistle

Anonymous

I want to learn to whistle,
I've always wanted to;
I fix my mouth to do it, but,
The whistle won't come through.

I think perhaps it's stuck, and so,
I try it once again;
Can people swallow whistles?
Where is my whistle then?

It's not easy to whistle on demand, but a lone whistler or a chorus of whistlers (whether proficient or attempting whistlers) adds to the effective presentation of this poem on the third or fourth reading.

Share:
Honeycut, Natalie. *Whistle Home.* Art by Annie Cannon. Orchard, 1993.

A caretaker whistles Dooley, the dog, home after a friendly apple-picking session.

The Girl Who Makes the Cymbals Bang

by X. J. Kennedy

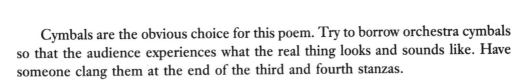

I'm the girl who makes the cymbals bang—
It used to be a boy
That got to play them in the past
Which always would annoy

Me quite a lot. Though I complained,
Our teacher Mister Cash
Said, "Sorry, girls don't have the strength
To come up with a crash."

"Oh, yeah?" said I. "Please give them here!"
And there and then, I slammed
Together those brass plates so hard
His eardrums traffic-jammed.

He gulped and gaped, and I could tell
His old ideas were bending—
So now me and my cymbals give
Each song a real smash ending.

Cymbals are the obvious choice for this poem. Try to borrow orchestra cymbals so that the audience experiences what the real thing looks and sounds like. Have someone clang them at the end of the third and fourth stanzas.

Here Comes the Band

by William Cole

The band comes booming down the street,
The tuba oomphs, the flutes tweet tweet;
The trombones slide, the trumpets blare,
The baton twirls up in the air.
There's "ooh's!" and "ahs!" and cheers and clapping—
And I can't stop my feet from tapping.

This poem calls for both a band (make-believe or real) and the crowd on the street, who clap and cheer.

Roadside Peddlers

by Monica Gunning

Roadside peddlers,
their tangerines strung on strings,
wait under bamboo lean-tos,
call out to passersby.

"Fresh fiiish,
sweet mangoes off me tree!
Nice ripe tangerines, Man,
yellow like the sun."

Roadside peddlers
holding up guineps
hurry to the windows
of buses and cars.

"This bunch sweeter!
You must try mine, Ma'am!"
and beam when they sell
even one bunch.

This poem takes place along the road somewhere in the Caribbean. Are there street merchants in your town? Maybe some of the children have tried selling lemonade from stands in their own neighborhood or bought ice cream from a vendor in the park and remember the rhythmic calls to draw attention to their products. Encourage them to recreate those persuasive cadences as they "sell" their exotic wares in this poem. The children will be curious to learn that the guinep is a small, green-skinned fruit, very popular in Jamaica, that is ripe during the summer months.

9

Prop Poetry

March in with a balloon bouquet. Hand out a souvenir. Unwrap a birthday present: All are ideas for presenting poetry using visuals. Prop poetry is particularly useful when you want to get the undivided attention of an active audience or an inattentive one, such as you might encounter at the local mall or the county fair. Props are a help, too, to people who find it difficult to memorize a poem. The text of the poem can be affixed to the back of a poster or object and read aloud. If you discover that you enjoy this show-and-tell poetry, you may find yourself tending to exclude simple reading or reciting from your presentations. It is wise to use these visuals sparingly since there is a danger that some quiet poems will be overwhelmed rather than enhanced by any visual distraction. You don't want children to pay more attention to the prop than the words and meaning of the poem. You also don't want to find that you are competing with yourself for bigger and more extravagant presentations. You may begin one day with a plush animal and find yourself another day marching in with a live elephant.

However, it is amusing to play with poetry in this fashion. As you become familiar with the poems throughout this book and with the selections in other collections, you will begin to think in terms of props as you go about your daily life. As I do, you may pick up a toilet plunger in your home and think, "This will be perfect for Shel Silverstein's poem." In the grocery store you'll begin to look at the merchandise not as dinner, but as accessories to tomorrow's poetry break.

Present any of these poems in the traditional fashion one day and with a prop another day. Let's define a prop as anything that visually augments the oral presentation. You can use original art, posters, or artifacts.

Pictures

The most common use of props is to show a picture, an illustration of the poem. Hold one up at the end of the poem or use several illustrations to visually express the entire poem as you recite. Sometimes a poem will have a punch line that works well with a picture held up on the final line of the poem.

Artifacts

My favorite poetry artifact is a toilet plunger to go with Shel Silverstien's "The Hat." On the last line of the poem I put a toilet plunger on my head. I often use this poem to demonstrate to workshop participants how little time it takes to recite a poem. This particular Silverstein poem takes only six seconds to recite. In addition to the asset of being quick to slip into a full day's schedule, it certainly would be memorable to a child if the teacher, librarian, principal or mayor wore a toilet plunger on his or her head. My toilet plunger was purchased in Baghdad, Iraq, in the *suq*, an outdoor/indoor market in the center of the city. It cost less than a dollar. If you are looking for a bargain, you can buy a plunger, with a handcarved handle, at a good price there—plus, of course, the cost of a trip to Iraq. When I was in Toronto, someone who had attended my workshops told me that because of me her shopping takes twice as long as it once did. Now, she is constantly searching through the bargain tables looking for poem- or story-related objects that she might like to exhibit or use in her presentations.

I understand. It's difficult to resist the "perfect" visual, even if you do have to carry it back to Vancouver from Fairbanks. Keep your collection of poetry props in one location if possible so that you can always reach into a box and pull out the perfect prop for the day's presentation. If you are very organized, you might keep an inventory of possible props and their location, updating it so that you can always look through the list for a last minute idea for the poetry break.

POEMS IN PROP POETRY

Balloon Man • Rose Fyleman

Extra! Extra! • Colin McNaughton

Paper Bag • Zaro Weil

Magnet • Valerie Worth

Mop and Broom • Dee Lillegard

Keep a Poem in Your Pocket • Beatrice Schenk deRegniers

Abracadabra • Mary Ann Hoberman

Soap Bubbles • Yoshiko Uchida

Gourd Have Mercy • Felice Lamport

How Do You Like to Go Up in a Swing? • Robert Louis Stevenson

President • Dee Anderson

Mother's Chocolate Valentine • Jack Prelutsky

Chocolate • Arnold Adoff

Nutty Chocolate Cookies • Pauline Watson

The Valentine • Linda Paulsen

Chocolate Cake • Nina Payne

Jump Rope Rhyme • Charlie Meehan

The Balloon Man

by Rose Fyleman

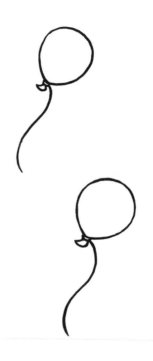

He always comes on market days,
   And holds balloons—a lovely bunch—
And in the market square he stays,
   And never seems to think of lunch.

They're red and purple, blue and green,
   And when it is a sunny day
Tho' carts and people get between
   You see them shining far away.

And some are big and some are small,
   All tied together with a string,
And if there is a wind at all
   They tug and tug like everything.

Some day perhaps he'll let them go
   And we shall see them sailing high,
And stand and watch them from below—
   They *would* look pretty in the sky!

    Balloons are the obvious souvenir to give when presenting this poem. Blow up the balloons and decorate the room or hold them in a bunch while you present.

Share:
Lenssen, Ann. *A Rainbow Balloon; A Book of Concepts*. Photos by author. Dutton, 1992.
Ross, Christine. *Lily and the Present*. Art by the author. Houghton, 1992.

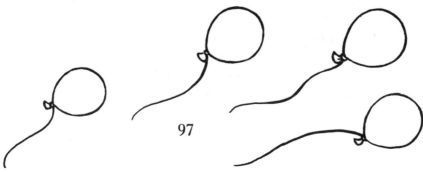

Extra! Extra!

by Colin McNaughton

"Extra! Extra! Read all about it!
Two men swindled! The latest news!"

"You there! Newsboy! Sell me a paper—
That's an offer I can't refuse!
Hey, there's nothing about a swindle!
Not one word or a why, where, whose!"

"Extra! Extra! Read all about it!
Three men swindled! The latest news!"

Copy the poem and place it inside a newspaper. Open the paper and read the poem. Several children can stand behind the presenter, all reading newspapers.

The Paper Bag

by Zaro Weil

Fill up a paper bag with
Spring sounds and
Open it in December

Fill up a paper bag with
Snow flurries and
Use them to decorate your bedroom.

Fill up a paper bag with
Ribbons and
Fly them when you want a word with the wind

Fill up a paper bag with
Winter quiet and
Open it when it's time to be alone

Fill up a paper bag with
Your favorite words and
Shake it till a good story comes out

Fill up a paper bag with
Secrets and
Share them with a friend every so often

Fill up a paper bag with
Velvet
Just to have it

Open a paper bag and mime the objects mentioned in the poem. Another way of presenting this poem is to have the children shut their eyes and "see" the items mentioned.

Share:
Thompson, Colin. *The Paper Bag Prince.* Art by author. Random, 1992.

Magnet

by Valerie Worth

This small
Flat horseshoe
Is sold for
A toy: we are
Told that it
Will pick up pins
And it does, time
After time; later
It lies about,
Getting its red
Paint chipped, being
Offered pins less
Often, until at
Last we leave it
Alone: then
It leads its own
Life, trading
Secrets with
The North Pole,
Reading
Invisible messages
From the sun.

Magnets can be given out as souvenirs or use this poem as an introduction to a demonstration of the magic of magnets.

Mop and Broom

by Dee Lillegard

Mop and Broom
by the light of the moon
dance around in the laundry room—
into the kitchen
all over the floor,
sweeping out spider and mouse
and more—
No two are happier
as they hop
than Mop and Broom,
Broom and Mop.

Two performers can dance with a mop and a broom as this poem is recited.

102

Keep a Poem in Your Pocket

by Beatrice Schenk de Regniers

Keep a poem in your pocket
and a picture in your head
and you'll never feel lonely
at night when you're in bed.

The little poem will sing to you
the little picture will bring to you
a dozen dreams to dance to you
at night when you're in bed.

So—
Keep a picture in your pocket
and a poem in your head
and you'll never feel lonely
at night when you're in bed.

The poem can be written on a sheet of paper that the presenter takes from her pocket, unfolds, and, after reading the poem, returns to her pocket. While reciting the last verse, she can pat her pocket, then pull out a small photo. The presenter should try to wear a smock or other clothing that day with generous pockets from which objects can be extracted easily.

Share:

Merriam, Eve. *What Can You Do with a Pocket?* Art by Harriet Sherman. Knopf, 1964.

Objects in your pocket are keyed to winsome activities.

Abracadabra

by Mary Ann Hoberman

Abracadabra
The zebra is black
Abracadabra
The zebra is white
Abracadabra
The zebra is dark
Abracadabra
The zebra is light

   Is it black striped with white?
   Is it white striped with black?
   Is it striped from the front?
   Is it striped from the back?

Abracadabra
It's ink over snow
Abracadabra
It's snow over ink
Abracadabra
Does anyone know
Abracadabra
What do you think?

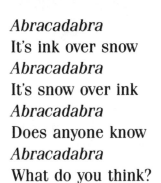

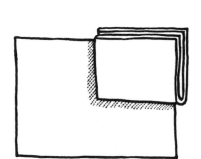

Pair this poem with the perfect magic-trick prop:
The Cut-and-Restored-Zebra Paper Tear.
You need:

A picture of an all-white horse.

A picture of an all-black horse.

A picture of a zebra.

Glue

How to:

Fold the picture of the zebra into quarters concealing the image. Glue an unfolded edge of the folded picture to the right-hand side of the back of the picture of the black horse. (If you are left-handed, attach it to the left side.) Place the picture of the white horse over the black one.

Patter:

Recite "Abracadabra" while alternately placing the black horse and the white horse picture in front. When you reach the last verse, place the white horse over the black horse, holding the folded picture of the striped zebra with your right hand, so that you won't tear that by mistake. Start tearing up the two solid-color horse pictures, keeping your right hand over the folded picture. When the pictures are torn up, let the torn strips slip into your right hand, turn the folded picture over and use your left hand to unfold the picture of the striped zebra. The torn pictures will still be held in your right hand. Simply put the torn paper in your pocket while the children are marveling at the fully restored black-and-white zebra. You won't be able to show the back of the zebra picture because there will be a piece of the black horse picture glued to it.

Share:

McCully, Emily Arnold. *The Amazing Felix*. Art by the author. Putnam, 1993.

Felix practices a magic trick and performs in place of his father, a famous pianist.

Soap Bubbles

by Yoshiko Uchida

The soap bubble man
Can blow a
Bubble as
Big as your head.

He can blow
A little tiny bubble
Inside a
Great big bubble.

He can make
Bubble chains
And even
Square bubbles,
Yes, he can.

The bubbles
Soon vanish
And so does he.

But he left me
Some words
To keep
After he was
Gone.

"Float peacefully
Through life,"
He said.

That's a lot
Harder to do
Than it sounds.

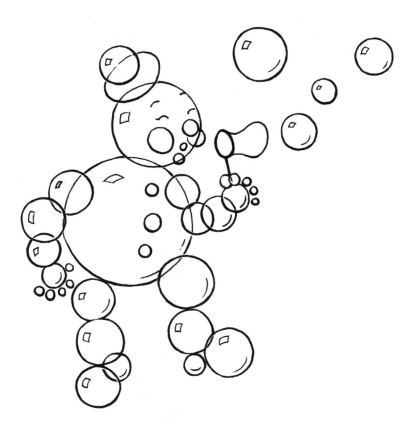

This poem will give you the perfect excuse to play with bubbles. Make soap bubbles from liquid detergent or buy commercial bubble solution, bring inexpensive bubble wands, and let your group experiment with bubblemania.

106

Gourd Have Mercy

by Felicia Lamport

If there's anything more galling than the crop
    that flopped,
  It's the crop that has too fulsomely succeeded.
Which can make you start to think it would
    be wise to opt
  For a garden that's unplanted and unweeded—
    A feeling that increases at a stiffer rate
    The moment your zucchini vines proliferate.

For they fructify so freely that they summon
    shades
  Of terror from "The Sorcerer's Apprentice"
When the gourds keep coming at you in such
    cavalcades
  That you're sure you'll soon become *non
    compos mentis.*
    The teeniest zucchini can, in one day
      flat,
    Expand to the dimension of a baseball bat.

You can stew it, fry it, roast it, you can serve
    it raw,
  Or even try it stuffed into a blini,
But there's little hope of finding a receptive maw:
  However thin it's sliced, it's still zucchini.
    So pull up every second vine that starts
      to sprout—
  The zucchini's going to get you if you don't
    watch out!

Serve sliced raw zucchini as a treat with this poem.

Share:

Hickman, Martha Whitmore. *And God Created Squash: How the World Began.* Art by Giuliano Ferri. Whitman, 1993.

God creates people, animals, and . . . squash.

Hunter, C.W. *The Green Gourd: A North Carolina Folktale.* Art by Tony Griego. Putnam, 1992.

A merry chase ensues when "a fractious green gourd's fixin' to frump me good."

How Do You Like to Go Up in a Swing?

by Robert Louis Stevenson

How do you like to go up in a swing,
    Up in the air so blue?
Oh, I do think it the pleasantest thing
    Ever a child can do!

Up in the air and over the wall,
    Till I can see so wide,
Rivers and trees and cattle and all
    Over the countryside—

Till I look down on the garden green,
    Down on the roofs so brown—
Up in the air I go flying again,
    Up in the air and down!

Perfect for the playground: enjoy a poetry break near the swings.

President

by Dee Anderson

My dad says school's important;
It helps me learn and grow,
And if I work real hard in school,
Who knows how far I'll go?

He says if I do well in school,
I could be anything someday;
I even could be president
of the whole U.S. of A.

I hate to tell my dad he's wrong,
But he's making a mistake.
I *never* could be president;
You see, I am a snake.

On the last line open a can of spring-snakes, available from a magic shop.

A Souvenir Mini-Program on: CHOCOLATE

Mother's Chocolate Valentine

by Jack Prelutsky

I bought a box of chocolate hearts,
a present for my mother,
they looked so good I tasted one,
and then I tried another.

They both were so delicious
that I ate another four,
and then another couple,
and then a dozen more.

I couldn't seem to stop myself,
I nibbled on and on,
before I knew what happened
all the chocolate hearts were gone.

I felt a little guilty,
I was stuffed down to my socks,
I ate my mother's valentine . . .
I hope she likes the box.

Recite while holding a candy box. Mime the action and on the last line show that the box is empty. Think of the preparation for this poem: eating the chocolates to empty the box.

Chocolate

by Arnold Adoff

CHOCOLATE
CHOCOLATE
    i
love
   you so
     i
want
    to
marry
    you
    and
live
   forever
      in the
      flavor
of your
   brown.

Nutty Chocolate Cookies

by Pauline Watson

Preheat oven to 375 degrees.
You will need: bowl, stirring spoon, greased cookie sheet,
        measuring cups and spoons, teaspoon.

1/2 cup shortening	1 teaspoon salt
3/4 cup brown sugar, firmly packed	1/2 tspn baking soda
1 1/2 cups flour	2 tblsns. water
1 egg	1/2 cup chopped nuts
	1 cup chocolate bits

Mix to the tune of "She'll Be Comin' Round the Mountain":

Cream the shortening with the sugar, cream it well.
Stir the mixture with a spoon, now give a yell.
Add the flour to the bowl;
Add the egg as you are told.
Stir the mixture with a spoon and add the salt.

Mix the soda with the water, mix it well;
Add the mixture to the bowl, now give a yell.
Add the nuts and chocolate bits;
Stir as if you're having fits.
Stir the mixture in the bowl, as you are told.

Take a teaspoon of the mixture and be neat.
Drop it carefully upon a cookie sheet.
Now repeat until you clean up;
Bake the cookies till they brown up.
Bake the cookies till they brown up—fit to eat.

Bake 10 to 12 minutes. Makes 30 cookies.

The Valentine

by Linda G. Paulsen

I drew a heart and painted it red.
Carefully printed what it said.
Glued on paper lace and then,
Shyly gave it to my friend.

And what do you think happened next?
As I stood (both knees 'bout flexed),
My friend smiled and gave me this
Great big, giant, chocolate KISS!

Chocolate Cake

by Nina Payne

Chocolate cake
chocolate cake
that's the one
I'll help you make
Flour soda
salt are sifted
butter sugar
cocoa lifted
by the eggs
then mix the whole
grease the pans
I'll lick the bowl
Chocolate caked
chocolate caked
that's what I'll be
when it's baked.

Jump Rope Rhyme

by Charlie Meehan

Chocolate ice cream,
Chocolate cake,
Chocolate shake,
Chocolate bagels,
Chocolate steak,
Make a chocolate belly ache!
Faster!
Chocolateicecream,
Chocolatecake,
Chocolateshake,
Chocolatebagels,
Chocolatesteak,
Makeachocolatebellyache!

Use these poems individually or as an entire program featuring chocolate. You'll be tempted to accompany this section with a treat. Why not? A chocolate kiss fits perfectly with this theme. And you might want to create a bulletin board of discarded chocolate candy wrappers featuring the poems.

Share:

Jaspersohn, William. *Cookies*. Photos by author. Macmillan, 1993.

A photo essay shows how chocolate chip cookies are made at a factory.

Obligado, Lilian. *The Chocolate Cow*. Art by the author. Simon & Schuster, 1993.

Melody the cow is saved from being sold when she becomes the "poster cow" for a chocolate company in Switzerland.

10

 Think About It

It's fun to find humorous rhymes and poems and think of amusing ways to present them, but the ultimate presentation is to let the words of the poem do the work. Any poem in this book can, of course, just be recited or read aloud with great success, but the poems in this section will make you stop and think.

It isn't necessary to force your listeners into some sort of reaction by asking questions or insisting on a written response. Simply read the poem aloud as the day's choice for the poetry break. If you read the poem aloud more than once, your listeners will have a better opportunity to understand the meaning of the poem and will be able to react on their own. Don't expect children to articulate their feelings immediately. They might never say anything about the poem, but, we hope, they will think about it on the way home from the library, while taking a bath, or when they are alone in bed.

If you find that you can't resist using one of these as an oral or written exercise, try to avoid asking questions on the first reading. Give the children time to absorb the poem.

You might want to alternate selections in this group with those that have a lighter theme. And, of course, you will find many choices, in addition to these examples, that fall into the category of "thinking" poems.

Thought-provoking poems might remind you of personal stories that you want to share as introductions. It's not always necessary to introduce a poem, but these poems are the sort that bring past vignettes to mind, or remind you of a pertinent personal experience you'll want to relate. Using the "personal" introduction is another way to involve your audience. Most children—and adults, too—enjoy a quick glimpse into the memories and lives of their leader. Obviously, you don't want to overwhelm a six-line poem with a long, involved story. However, a short preliminary reflection may help your audience to define their own feelings about a particular poem. When it's their turn to give the poetry break, they may introduce a poem that was used another day, but personalize it with their own introduction.

The introductions used with these poems relate to my own experiences, but they should give you a direction for composing yours.

THINK ABOUT IT POEMS

Dog Lovers • Spike Milligan

A Red Morning Sky • Issa

Two People I Want to Be Like • Eve Merriam

The Picture • Jeff Moss

Why are all of these flowers in bloom? • Kazue Mizumara

How Do You Say Goodbye? • Lois Simmie

No Difference • Shel Silverstein

Happy Birthday, Dilroy • John Agard

Trinity Place • Phyllis McGinley

In the Museum • Charlotte Zolotow

I'm Goin' to Pray for Peace • Beth Wilson

The Rabbit • Alan Brownjohn

Dog Lovers

by Spike Milligan

So they bought you
And kept you in a
Very good home
Central heating
TV
A deep freeze
A *very* good home—
No one to take you
For that lovely long run—
But otherwise
"A *very* good home."
They fed you Pal and Chum
But not that lovely long run,
Until, mad with energy and boredom
You escaped—and ran and ran and ran
Under a car.
Today they will cry for you—
Tomorrow they will buy another dog.

We often see a cocker spaniel taking his morning walk with the owner. They both seem to enjoy their daily strolls, but I worry because the traffic on our street is fierce, and the owner never puts a leash on the dog. What if that cocker ran across the street after a cat?

Share:

Rosen, Michael J., ed. *Speak! Children's Book Illustrators Brag About Their Dogs*. Harcourt, 1993.

Forty-three illustrators write about and draw pictures of their dogs.

A Red Morning Sky

by Issa

A red morning sky,
For you, snail;
    Are you glad about it?

We recently moved from the West Coast of the United States, where we enjoyed the sunsets over the Pacific Ocean. Now, we live on the East Coast, and our apartment faces the Atlantic Ocean. Instead of sunsets, we watch the sunrises. Early in the morning, there are water birds floating on the sea, facing the sun. I wonder if they are telling each other about the glorious sunrise.

Two People I Want to Be Like

by Eve Merriam

That man
stuck in traffic
not pounding his fists againts the steering wheel
not trying to shift to the next lane
just
using the time
for a slow steady grin
of remembering
all the good unstuck times

and that woman
clerking in the supermarket
at rush hour
bagging bottles and cartons and boxes and
    jars and cans
punching it all out
slapping it all along
and leveling a smile
at everyone in the line.

I wish they were married to each other.

Maybe it's better they're not,
so they can pass their sweet harmony around.

    I used to commute to work in a big city. It was frustrating to be slowed down every morning and evening by gigantic traffic jams. I often amused myself by making up stories about the drivers in the cars that waited on either side of me on the freeway. You can try the same game when you ride a bus or subway daily. If you are a poet, you can put your speculations into words as Eve Merriam has done in this poem.

The Picture

by Jeff Moss

My Grandpa can't hear things as well as he used to,
He wears thick glasses to help him see.
When we ride in his car, he drives very slowly.
I feel his hand shake when he walks with me.

My dad has a box that's filled with old pictures,
In some of them Grandpa's as young as my Dad.
There's one where he's holding my Dad on his shoulders,
When I see that picture, sometimes I feel sad.

My Grandpa's not strong but he's kind and he's funny,
Still I know he'll never be younger again.
So sometimes I wish I could climb in that picture
And visit with Grandpa the way he was then.

We're not very organized in our house. If you start looking for something in the attic, you will discover boxes and boxes of unsorted family photos. Sometimes I sit on the floor and look through the photos, marveling at pictures of my mother holding my baby daughter. How strange that feels when both my mother and my daughter are so much older now.

Why are all of these flowers in bloom?

by Kazue Mizumara

Why are all of these flowers
In bloom? Don't they know
This house is for sale?

How Do You Say Goodbye?

by Lois Simmie

How do you say goodbye to a house
When you're moving forever on Saturday,
When you've lived there always—seven years,
And no matter what, they won't let you stay?

How do you say goodbye to a room
With its just-right walls and corners and nooks,
With its Snoopy curtains, all faded and blue,
And shelves for your toys, and fishtank, and books?

How do you say goodbye to the tree
That grew up so tall by your bedroom window,
That dances its leaves on your yellow walls
And lulls you to sleep whenever the wind blows?

How do you say goodbye to a street
Where you know all the hedges and places to hide,
The back alley fence where you broke your arm,
And the hill at the end where you used to slide?

I wish I could move this house and this tree—
This yard—this street—these swings;
My friends can all come and visit me,
But how do you say goodbye to things?

Our family has moved more than a dozen times. When I leave a house, I always wonder how the house feels about our leaving. Does it wonder who its new owners will be? Is it hoping that they will have children or a dog—or would it rather house a quiet older couple?

Share:

Ryder, Joanne. *The Goodbye Walk.* Art by Deborah Haeffele. Dutton, 1993.

In this picture essay, a young girl is saying goodbye to the landmarks of summer and storing memories in her mind.

No Difference

by Shel Silverstein

Small as a peanut
Big as a giant,
We're all the same size
When we turn off the light.

Rich as a sultan,
Poor as a mite,
We're all worth the same
When we turn off the light.

Red, black or orange,
Yellow or white,
We all look the same
When we turn off the light.

So maybe the way
To make everything right
Is for God to just reach out
And turn off the light!

Our neighborhood is a wonderful place. On any day you can hear five or six different languages. Our neighbors are from all over the world and I like to guess where they lived before they came to America. It would be so dull and boring if we all looked and acted the same. I love to watch and listen to the children playing together, even when they don't understand each other. I guess everyone can understand fun.

Share:
Spier, Peter. *People*. Art by the author. Doubleday, 1980.
> In an oversized picture book, Spier celebrates the differences among the people on the planet.

Happy Birthday, Dilroy

by John Agard

My name is Dilroy.
I'm a little black boy
and I'm eight today.

My birthday cards say
it's great to be eight
and they sure right
coz I got a pair of skates
I want for a long long time.

My birthday cards say,
Happy Birthday, Dilroy!
But, Mummy, tell me why
they don't put a little boy
that looks a bit like me.
Why the boy on the card so white?

When I was a little girl it seemed as though all my favorite books were about boys. Where were the girls? Today, there are books written about girls as well as boys, and many authors and artists strive to reflect the different races, ethnic groups, and cultures who live in the United States. It is nice to see someone like yourself in a book, on a card, or a poster.

Trinity Place

by Phyllis McGinley

The pigeons scan with disfavor the men who sit
     there,
  Listless in sun or shade. The pigeons sidle
Between the gravestones with shrewd, industrious
     motions.
  The pigeons are busy. It is only the men who
     are idle.

The pigeons sharpen their beaks on the stones, and
     they waddle
  In dignified search of their proper, their daily
     bread.
Their eyes are small with contempt for the men
     on the benches.
  It is only the men who are hungry. The pigeons
     are fed.

   This morning I watched an old man who seems to have no home feeding the seagulls on the beach. I wondered where he found food for the birds when he obviously didn't have much for himself.

In the Museum

by Charlotte Zolotow

The horse from 200 B.C.
is made of stone,
but the way he holds his head
shows
someone long ago
loved a horse like him.
though now
both horse and sculptor
                    are dead.

On our living room wall there is a sampler stitched by my great aunt. At the bottom there is a date stitched in many colors that are faded from the sunlight that strikes the sampler in the morning. My great aunt has been dead for many years, but I know that she made the sampler over a one hundred years ago. Maybe I should paint a picture or make a quilt. It would be nice to be remembered a hundred years from now.

125

I'm Goin' to Pray for Peace

by Beth Wilson

I don't like war.
I saw some pictures on TV.
An' it was terrible!
When I say my prayers
I'm goin' to pray for peace.

Sometimes, when I watch the news on television I wish that I were the winner of the tennis match that's being shown. But other times, I see what is happening in a war someplace. Then I wish that I could do something to make the world a happier place.

Share:

Dolphin, Laurie. *Oasis of Peace*. Photos by Ben Dolphin. Scholastic, 1993.

Grades 3–5. An Arab boy and a Jewish boy live in the same community near Jerusalem.

Houston, Gloria. *But No Candy*. Art Lloyd Bloom. Philomel, 1992.

A little girl waits for the war to end.

Tsuchiya, Yukio. *Faithful Elephants: A True Story of Animals, People, and War*. Art by Ted Lewin. Translated by Tomoko Tsuchiya Dykes. Houghton, 1988.

The fate of the elephants in the Tokyo zoo revolves around the war.

The Rabbit

by Alan Brownjohn

We are going to see the rabbit.
We are going to see the rabbit.
Which rabbit? people say.
Which rabbit? ask the children.
Which rabbit?
The only rabbit,
The only rabbit in England,
Sitting behind a barbed-wire fence
Under the floodlights, neon lights,
Sodium lights,
Nibbling grass
On the only patch of grass
In England, in England
(Except the grass by the hoardings
Which doesn't count.)
We are going to see the rabbit
And we must be there on time.

First we shall go by escalator,
Then we shall go by underground,
And then we shall go by motorway
And then by helicopterway,
And the last ten yards we shall have to go
On foot.

And now we are going.
All the way to see the rabbit.
We are nearly there,
We are longing to see it,

And so is the crowd
Which is here in thousands
With mounted policemen
And big loudspeakers
And bands and banners,
And everyone has come a long way.
But soon we shall see it
Sitting and nibbling
The blades of grass
On the only patch of grass
In—but something has gone wrong!

Why is everyone so angry?
Why is everyone jostling
And slanging and complaining?

The rabbit has gone,
Yes, the rabbit has gone.
He has actually burrowed down into the earth
And made himself a warren, under the earth,
Despite all these people.
And what shall we do?
What *can* we do?

It is all a pity, you must be disappointed,
Go home and do something else for today,
Go home again, go home for today.
For you cannot hear the rabbit, under the earth,
Remarking rather sadly to himself, by himself,
As he rests in his warren, under the earth:
'It won't be long, they are bound to come,
They are bound to come and find me, even here.'

I used to ride my horse in a meadow near the sea. Every morning I saw rabbits, birds, skunks, coyotes, and once in a while, even a fox. There are houses in that meadow now. I'm sure the people who live there would be annoyed if rabbits ate their flower gardens and foxes roamed their backyards, but where did those animals go?

11

Write It

Listening to a poem can be compared to listening to music. The more you hear a poem the more you will appreciate it. Sometimes when you attend a concert, the music inspires thoughts of other times and places. Poetry can have the same effect on your senses. A line from a poem, the subject of the poem, or just the rhythm of the words can inspire your own creative writing.

It is a good idea to have paper and pen ready so that, whenever one of these stray thoughts occurs, you can write it down and, at a later date, develop it into a story, essay, or poem of your own. If your students are keeping journals, they may already have the habit of writing fragments of ideas, quotes, and thoughts in their journals. The journal habit is a useful one to develop: not only does it make writing easier to have the idea already in written form, but the notes often trigger memories that can become further inspiration to writing.

When we moved recently, my daughter found journals that she had kept in elementary school. I was finally allowed to read some of the entries. Hilary had recorded fragmentary thoughts and composed short rhymes and longer essays that revealed her thinking when she was in fourth grade. She really writes quite well now. I wonder if using a journal as a friend helped develop this talent.

Suggest to your students, reading club, or library group that the poetry break may inspire them to write or tell something that they thought of when the poem was presented. You will not always have the time to sit down and write something on the spot, but some poems are more provocative than others, and when these are presented, time should be alloted, if at all possible, for developing a writing activity.

Use these poems throughout the year as offerings in the poetry break. When you have a bit more time you might repeat the poem and suggest that it be used to spark children's own writing. Don't expect everyone to participate. Writers—amateurs or professionals—cannot write on demand. However, as an exercise, these choices may provide an inspiration or direction for some would-be writers or poets.

Since the stated and true purpose of this book is to bring children to poetry in a pleasurable way, don't try to key an activity to every poetry break; try to keep poetry-activity extensions optional. Not everyone enjoys writing, and you don't want to have anyone dislike the poetry because now they *have* to write something. Although it may seem obvious to write a poem when you are inspired by a poem, it may be more practical or comfortable to write an essay, story or informational piece. Try to keep any writing time as open and as flexible as possible. The poetry break should seem to be "just for fun" and so should the writing time. Of course, both activities will also give your children a deeper appreciation for and more comfort with poetry and writing.

The poems in this section have been selected as possible springboards to writing, but browse through the other chapters and find selections that may also appeal to you.

WRITE IT POEMS

Blum • Dorothy Aldis

Write a Petition • Siv Widerberg

Halfway Down • A. A. Milne

Packing Up • Grace Cornell Tall

A New Friend • Marjorie Allen Anderson

I'm an Ant • Pam Brewster

The Alien • Julie Holder

Postman, Postman • Arnold Lobel

Elephant for Sale • Maurice Poe

Grocery Oasis • Ruth Haq

By Myself • Eloise Greenfield

The Limerick's Lively to Write • David McCord

Write a Limerick Now • David McCord

Blum

by Dorothy Aldis

Dog means dog. And cat means cat.
And there are lots of words like that.

A cart's a cart to pull or push.
A leaf's a leaf on tree or bush.

But there's another word I say
When I am left alone to play.

The word is Blum. Blum is a word
That very few have ever heard.

It is very nice to hum.
Or you can shout it: BLUM BLUM BLUM.

But shout or whisper, hum or sing,
It doesn't mean a single thing.

List your own favorite words on the chalkboard. Recite them as you would a poem. Try rearranging the words to make a more poetic grouping of the words' sounds and meanings.

Write a Petition

by Siv Widerberg

You may not believe it
but we've got a soccer field now
behind Andy and Hugo's house,
beside the grocery store
in our town outside Stockholm, Sweden
A really neat soccer field
with goalposts and everything
"Write a petition
and tape it on the door
of every building!" said a big guy I know
So that's what we did
We want a soccer field!
we wrote
And then: Anders Andersson,
Leif Lundin, Hugo Blomkvist,
Gertrud Nilsson (who's me)
and all the others
Last Tuesday we got it,
behind Andy and Hugo's house,
beside the grocery store
and with white goalposts

Try it yourself
and you'll see:
Write down what you want on top,
and then a whole bunch of names underneath it

Anyhow we got
our soccer field
that way
even if you don't believe it!

Discuss a project that you would like to see happen in your neighborhood. Can you help the idea become reality by reaching a politician or a government agency? Write a petition, gather signatures, and send it to someone who can make your goal possible.

Share:
Lawler, Rick. *How to Write to World Leaders*. MinRef Press, 1990.
Lewis, Barbara A. *Kid's Book of Social Action*. Free Spirit, 1991.

Halfway Down

by A. A. Milne

Halfway down the stairs
Is a stair
Where I sit.
There isn't any
Other stair
Quite like
It.
I'm not at the bottom,
I'm not at the top;
So this is the stair
Where
I always
Stop.

Halfway up the stairs
Isn't up,
And isn't down.
It isn't in the nursery,
It isn't in the town.
And all sorts of funny thoughts
Run round my head:
"It isn't really
Anywhere!
It's somewhere else
Instead!"

What is your favorite place to sit? What is your favorite place to read a book? Describe a favorite place.

Packing Up

by Grace Cornell Tall

Winter,
Put your things away!
Into your storebox
Let there go
The myriad flakes of whirling snow.
Pack up the winds
That sway the trees
And fold them neatly.
Over these,
Pile the layers
Of ice and frost.
One by one, stack on stack,
Put the crystal icicles back—
Let none be lost!
When all are in, shut the box,
And turn the key, and snap the locks.
Then, leave a note for all to read:
WINTER HAS GONE TO SPRING AND SEED

The rich detail in this poem makes the image of winter's "accessories" strong and vivid. How would you personify other seasons or natural phenomena?

A New Friend

by Marjorie Allen Anderson

They've taken in the furniture;
I watched them carefully.
I wondered, "Will there be a child
Just right to play with me?"

So I peeked through the garden fence
(I couldn't wait to see).
I found the little boy next door
Was peeking back at me.

This poem is written from the point of view of the established neighbor as a moving van pulls into his neighborhood. Write about what the new boy might be thinking as he arrives at his new home.

I'm an Ant

by Pam Brewster

I'm an ant
and a gi-ant.
I'm a gi-ant
to an ant,
but I'm an ant
to a gi-ant.

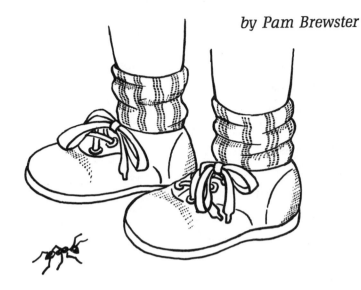

Write how you might react to an everyday situation if you were an ant?

Share:

Hepworth, Cathi. *Antics! An Alphabetic Anthology*. Putnam, 1992.

Each letter of the alphabet features a word and picture with the word "ant" in it.
Van Allsburg, Chris. *Two Bad Ants*. Art by author. Houghton, 1988.

The Alien

by Julie Holder

The alien
Was round as the moon
Five legs he had
And his ears played a tune.
His hair was pink
And his knees were green,
He was the funniest thing I'd seen.
As he danced in the door
Of his strange spacecraft,
He looked at me—
And laughed and laughed!

How would it feel to be an "alien" in a new school, new neighborhood, new country?

Share:
Bradman, Tony. *It Came From Outer Space.* Art by Carol Wright. Dial, 1992.

Postman, Postman

by Arnold Lobel

Postman, postman,
Ring my bell.
You are here
And all is well.
Postman, postman,
Bring my mail,
Let me serve you
Cakes and ale.
The day was sad,
But now it's better . . .
A friend has written me a letter.

Write a letter to a friend, real or imagined.

Elephant for Sale

by Maurice Poe

Elephant for sale!
Elephant for sale!
One big, beautiful
Elephant for sale!

He'll tell you a story
When you go to bed.
He'll fluff your pillow
And pat your head.

Elephant for sale!
Elephant for sale!
One big, beautiful
Elephant for sale!

He'll wash the dishes.
He'll mop the floor.
He'll carry out trash
And do lots more.

Elephant for sale!
Elephant for sale!
One big, beautiful
Elephant for sale!

He'll tell you a joke.
He'll sing you a song.
He'll read you a story
That's not too long.

Elephant for sale!
Elephant for sale!
One big, beautiful
Elephant for sale!

Mom says to sell him.
She says sell him right now.
She doesn't believe
He's an overgrown cow.

Elephant for sale!
Elephant for sale!
One big, beautiful
Elephant for sale!

I want to keep him
But Mom says, "No!"
And that's the reason
He has to go.

Elephant for sale!
Elephant for sale!
One big, beautiful
Elephant for sale!

143

Write a newspaper or magazine ad aimed at selling an unusual pet.

Share:

Blumberg, Rhoda. *Jumbo*. Art by Jonathan Hunt. Bradbury, 1992.

> Jumbo the elephant leaves his home in Africa and begins a career as a circus performer for P. T. Barnum.

Kipling, Rudyard. *The Elephant's Child*. Art by Emily Bolam. Dutton, 1992.

> The story of how the elephant got his trunk is the classic tale by Rudyard Kipling, accompanied by bright art.

McClung, Robert M. *America's First Elephant*. Art by Marilyn Janovitz. Morrow, 1991.

> Kandi is the very first elephant to be exhibited in America, arriving in 1796 and leading a parade in New York City.

Sierra, Judy. *The Elephant's Wrestling Match*. Art by Brian Pinkney. Dutton, 1992.

> An elephant is defeated by a tiny bat in a story from the Bulu of Africa.

Grocery Oasis

by Ruth Haq

When we're tired of tramping on hot concrete
That toasts our sneakers
And roasts our feet,
And the sidewalk sizzles,
And the pavement shimmers
With wavy wiggles of radiant heat,

We come to the welcome door
Of the air-conditioned
Grocery store.
What soothing coolness,
What frigid freshness—
From desert sand to oasis floor!

Let's stay all day,
Let's spend a while
In the frozen juice
And ice cream aisle!
Choosing greens
Will be specially nice—
We can dip our hands
In the chips of ice.

Let's not go out again on the street
To the sizzling sidewalk and hot concrete;
We'll be scorched if we stay in that heat anymore—
Let's wait for night in the grocery store!

What sort of store would you choose to visit if it were cold outside?

By Myself

by Eloise Greenfield

When I'm by myself
And I close my eyes
I'm a twin
I'm a dimple in a chin
I'm a room full of toys
I'm a squeaky noise
I'm a gospel song
I'm a gong
I'm a leaf turning red
I'm a loaf of brown bread
I'm a whatever I want to be
An anything I care to be
And when I open my eyes
What I care to be
Is me

If you couldn't be you, who would you be? Why?

The Limerick's Lively to Write

by David McCord

The limerick's lively to write:
Five lines to it—all nice and tight.
    Two long ones, two trick
    Little short ones, then quick
As a flash here's the last one in sight.

Write a Limerick Now

by David McCord

Write a limerick now. Say there was
An old man of some place, what he does,
    Or perhaps what he doesn't,
    Or isn't or wasn't.
Want help with it? Give me a buzz.

David McCord gives you directions in the first of these two poems to help you write a limerick. Try one.

The form in quick review: A five line poem. The first, second, and fifth lines rhyme and each has three metric feet (eight to ten syllables); the third and fourth lines rhyme and have two feet apiece (five to seven syllables). Limericks are usually humorous and while many of them are anonymous, the poet Edward Lear helped bring them to just fame.

Not interested in being confined to an exact form? Write about not wanting to write a limerick.

Share:

Lobel, Arnold. *The Book of Pigricks*. Art by the author. Harper, 1983.

    These limericks all feature pigs.

Livingston, Myra Cohn. *Lots of Limericks*. Art by Rebecca Perry. Macmillan, 1991.

    Selection of popular limericks.

12

Partners

"I can't have my first graders wandering around by themselves," may be your reaction to having a child act as the poetry break person. "Besides, won't they feel shy about bursting into and interrupting Mrs. Robbins's class with a poetry break?" You may find it practical to send two people on a journey around the school, and your poetry break presenters may feel more comfortable visiting classrooms and departments in pairs.

One person can be the speaker while the other holds the poetry break sign and introduces the poem. Two children can recite together, or they might each present a poem—perhaps on the same topic. This will extend the daily poetry break into a mini-theme program.

The poems you choose may be entirely unrelated, or they can be written by the same poet, or represent two different poets' views on the same subject. For a smoother and more professional presentation, the poetry pair should discuss and practice their deliveries. They will have to decide how best to introduce the theme and who will present first, as well as where it might be most advantageous to stand while presenting. Children often recite their selections with aplomb, but giggle with insecurity deciding who should go first and where to stand. Try to work out the logistics in the beginning, so that each presenter feels poised and confident.

Authors are frequently asked where they get their ideas. One might also ask how so many poets focus on the same subject for their work. The answer seems to be the one so often given by authors: People write from their own experiences. You will find that there are poems about the weather, sports, animals and people in all kinds of anthologies. If you enjoy this counterpoint idea, use the subject index of this collection to search for more poems that can be paired or used in threesomes.

Here are a few poems selected as partners. Don't forget to use these as singles as well.

PARTNERS POEMS

Partners

Homework • Russell Hoban

Homework • Jane Yolen

Overdog • Tony Johnston

Foul Shot • Edwin A. Hoey

SCHOOL DAYS

The Last Day of School

by Jack Prelutsky

On the last day of school
I was tickled to bits,
I hopped on my desk
and had six sorts of fits,
I was so glad to see
my vacation begin
that I practically wriggled
right out of my skin.
I rolled on the floor
and I leaped through the air,
I honked like a goose
and I roared like a bear,
I wiggled my ears
and I brayed like a mule,
that's what I did
on the last day of school.

Boring

by Jack Prelutsky

By the time that August ended
I was feeling sort of blue,
I was bored with skates and Frisbees,
climbing trees was boring too,
I was sick of running races,
throwing any sort of ball,
there simply wasn't anything
I cared to do at all.

It was boring, boring, boring
just to hear my parents say,
"Turn off the television, please,
and go outside and play."

I was glad to see September,
when vacation finally ends,
and glad to be back here again
in class with all my friends.

These two are perfect for a back-to-school program or for the last poetry break of the school year. They also showcase the talent of one popular poet.

ESCALATORS

Alligator on the Escalator

by Eve Merriam

Through the revolving door
Of a department store
There slithered an alligator.

When he came to the escalator,
He stepped upon the track with great dexterity;
His tail draped over the railing,
And he clicked his teeth with glee:
    "Yo, I'm off on the escalator,
    Excited as I can be!
    It's a *moving* experience,
    As you can plainly see.
    On the moving stair I go anywhere,
    I rise to the top
    Past outerwear, innerwear,
    Dinnerwear, thinnerwear—
    Then down to the basement with bargains
       galore,
    Then back on the track to the top once more!
    Oh, I may ride the escalator
    Until closing time or later,
    So tell the telephone operator
    To call Mrs. Albert Q. Alligator
    And tell her to take a hot mud bath
    And not to wait up for me!"

Ethel Earl

by Doug MacLeod

A little girl
called Ethel Earl
would ride the escalator,
and there she'd play
till, one sad day,
the escalator ate 'er.

She disappeared,
felt rather weird,
and tumbled out much later
all trembling
resembling
a crinkle-cut potater.

After reading these poems in tandem once, you might want to draw a girl on a sheet of newsprint and an alligator on a second sheet. Accordion pleat both sheets to represent the escalator. Open the pictures up at the end of the poems revealing Ethel amd Mr. Albert Q. Alligator.

CATERPILLARS

Message from a Caterpillar

by Lilian Moore

Don't shake this
bough.
Don't try to
wake me
now.

In this cocoon
I've work to
do.
Inside this silk
I'm changing
things.

I'm worm-like now
but in this
dark
I'm growing
wings.

Caterpillar

by Jack Prelutsky

Today he left his warm cocoon
And sadly ventured forth.
He'd hoped to be a butterfly,
but found himself a moth.

To turn these into prop poems, make two simple paper cocoons, a butterfly, and a moth. At the end of the poem pull out the appropriate creature.

Share:
Carle, Eric. *The Very Hungry Caterpillar*. Art by the author. Putnam, 1981.

A very hungry caterpillar eats through the days of the week.
French, Vivian. *Caterpillar, Caterpillar*. Art by Charlotte Voake. Candlewick, 1993.

A little girl and her grandfather watch the life cycle of a caterpillar.
Merrill, Jean. *The Girl Who Loved Caterpillars*. Art by Floyd Cooper. Philomel, 1992.

A twelfth-century Japanese girl prefers to study caterpillars and other small creatures rather than be courted by wealthy suitors.

All Star Boys

by Lynn Joseph

Jasmine and me want to play cricket
with the All Star Boys
in their spanking white shirts
and high knee socks
and their cricket bats
perched like machetes
on their wide shoulders.

But the batsman says, "Girls
cahn bat no cork ball."
And everyone laughs.
The bowler hollers, "Girls
cahn knock down wickets."
And everyone screams.
But me and Jasmine dohn forget
and when we grow up we'll have
a cricket team
with no discrimination!

Ebonee

Sharon Bell Mathias

All this hoopla
so much noise
just 'cause a girl's on the team
with us boys

People excited
clapping hands
calling EBONEE! EBONEE!
back and forth in the stands

Ebonee sits on the bench
quiet all the while
helmet pulled down over cornrows
and not one smile

Cute somebody called her
this week past
cute, I don't know
what Ebonee is—is fast

Ebonee's magic
does everything right
a running back
who's outta sight

These two work well read aloud, but also might be amusing for several students
to present as a team of girl cricketeers (see if someone has a cricket bat to exhibit)
and a lone girl wearing a football helmet.

COLORS

Chameleon

by Alan Brownjohn

I can think sharply
and I can change:
my colours cover a considerable range.

I can be some mud by
an estuary,
I can be a patch on the bark of a tree.

I can be green grass
or a little thin stone
—or if I really want to be left alone,

I can be a shadow . . .
What I am on your
multi-coloured bedspread, I am not quite sure.

The Color-Eater

by Constance Levy

Sunset mixed this recipe:
Orange and grape and raspberry,
Folded in and spread between
Lemonade and nectarine.
Too, too tempting
Don't you think
All that orange and
All that pink,
All that purple,
All that yellow?
Who could blame
The hungry fellow?
Night came sniffing
Like a pup;
Licked it
Liked it
Lapped it up!

Of course, you always remember to announce the poet and title of the poems, but these two are good examples of how really important the title is. In both cases, the title helps the listener to understand the poem.

DADS

Who'd Be A Juggler

by Cicely Herbert

Last night, in front of thousands of people,
he placed a pencil on his nose
and balanced a chair upright on it
while he spun a dozen plates behind his back.
Then he slowly stood on his head to read a book
at the same time as he transferred the lot
to the big toe of his left foot.
They said it was impossible.

This morning, in our own kitchen,
I asked him to help with the washing-up—
so he gets up, knocks over a chair,
trips over the cat, swears, drops the tray
and smashes the whole blooming lot!
You wouldn't think it was possible.

Dad and the Cat and the Tree

by Kit Wright

This morning a cat got
Stuck in our tree.
Dad said, 'Right, just
Leave it to me.'

The tree was wobbly,
The tree was tall.
Mum said, 'For goodness'
Sake don't fall!'

'Fall?' scoffed Dad,
'A climber like me?
Child's play, this is!
You wait and see.'

He got out the ladder
From the garden shed.
It slipped. He landed
In the flower bed.

'Never mind,' said Dad,
Brushing the dirt
Off his hair and his face
And his trousers and his shirt,

'We'll try Plan B. Stand
Out of the way!'
Mum said, 'Don't fall
Again, O.K.?'

'Fall again,' said Dad.
'Funny joke!'
Then he swung himself up
On a branch. It broke.

Dad landed *wallop*
Back on the deck.
Mum said, 'Stop it,
You'll break your neck!'

'Rubbish!' said Dad.
'Now we'll try Plan C.
Easy as winking
To a climber like me!'

Then he climbed up high
On the garden wall.
Guess what?
He *didn't fall*!

He gave a great leap
And he landed flat
In the crook of the tree-trunk—
Right on the cat!

The cat gave a yell
And sprang to the ground,
Pleased as Punch to be
Safe and sound.

So it's smiling and smirking,
Smug as can be,
But poor old Dad's
Still

Stuck
Up
The
Tree!

Both of these poems show good-humored views of two different dads.

165

CAUTIONS

Amanda!

by Robin Klein

Don't bite your nails, Amanda!
Don't hunch your shoulders, Amanda!
Stop that slouching and sit up straight,
Amanda!

(There is a languid, emerald sea,
where the sole inhabitant is me—
a mermaid drifting blissfully.)

Did you finish your homework, Amanda?
Did you tidy your room, Amanda?
I thought I told you to clean your shoes,
Amanda!

(I am an orphan, roaming the street,
I pattern soft dust with my hushed, bare feet.
The silence is golden, the freedom is sweet.)

Don't eat that chocolate, Amanda!
Remember your acne, Amanda!
Will you please look at me when I'm speaking to you,
Amanda!

(I am Rapunzel, I have not a care;
life in a tower is tranquil and rare;
I'll certainly *never* let down my bright hair!)

Stop that sulking at once, Amanda!
You're always so moody, Amanda!
Anyone would think that I nagged at you,
Amanda!

Baggage

by James S. Tippett

Don't forget the swimming suits;
Don't forget the thermos;
Don't forget the flashlight
And a lantern for the tent.

Don't forget the blankets;
Don't forget the sweaters;
"Don't forget" was all we heard
For days before we went.

Don't forget the lunch box!
Don't forget the Kodak!
Don't forget the camp stool
And don't forget the books!

"Don't forget! Don't forget!"
But when we came away
We did forget to bring with us
My father's fishing hooks.

Both poems show children being nagged by their parents, a theme children will
find familiar and funny.

PERFORMING

School Concert

by Marchette Chute

My family was the very proudest.
They said my singing was the loudest.

Last-minute Change

by Tony Johnston

The program was beautifully printed.
It says, Tommy Smith—"Polonaise."
So—
When I play them "Chopsticks" for my turn,
Won't everyone be amazed?

    Both of these are short. If you have time and talented students, two children might play their concert pieces on a piano or sing for the group.

RAINBOW

Fling Me a Rainbow

by Rebecca Caudill

"Fling me a rainbow!"
   I cry to the troubled sky,
And, look, she flings one.

Rhyming the Rainbow

by John Travers Moore

"Red," I said,
And "Orange," too,
"Yellow," next,
Then "Green" and "Blue,"
"Indigo,"
And "Violet" together—
All blend in
Down Rainbow-Weather!

   These rainbow poems can be extended with prisms that cast a rainbow, available at science shops, or they may be available to borrow from your school's science department.

SNEEZES

The Sneeze

by Sheree Fitch

I winked and I blinked
And my nose got itchy
And my eyes all watered
And my mouth went twitchy
I went AHHHH
I went AHHHH
I went AHHHH CHOOOOOO
And I blew
And I sneezed
Then I coughed
And I wheezed
And my brother said, "Oh, brother!"
And my mother said,
"GAZOONTIGHT!"
And father said, "Bless you!"
And I said, Ah . . . ah . . . ah . . .
AHHHHHHHHHHCHOOOOOOO!

Sneeze

by Maxine Kumin

There's a
sort of a
tickle
the size of a
nickel,
a bit like the
prickle

of a sweet-sour
pickle;
it's a
quivery
shiver
the shape of a
sliver,
like eels in a
river;
a kind of a
wiggle
that starts as a
jiggle
and joggles
its way to a
tease,
which I
cannot
suppress
any longer,
I guess,
so pardon me,
please,
while I sneeze.

These two can be presented by two partners or with a larger cast. For Sheree Fitch's "The Sneeze," you might have different children portray the "I," brother, mother, and father, each saying their lines, or let the audience join in on the actual sneeze.

Share:
Avalos, Cecilia. *The Goat Who Couldn't Sneeze*. Art by Vivi Escrivá. Scott Foresman, 1993

Fish

by Jeanne Steig

Of all the million kinds of fish,
There is not one will grant a wish
The way, in fairy tales, they used to.
Beg all you like, they just refuse to.

They don't hand out enchanted castles,
Nor golden swords with fancy tassels.
No prophecies! No sage advice!
Fish of today belong on ice.

Goldfish

by Kaye Starbird

I wonder about the thoughts and goals
Of goldfish living in goldfish bowls.

A goldfish drifts throuh his fishbowl greenery
And never mentions the lovely scenery
Or says he's really enthusiastic
About his pebbles of gay green plastic.

He never raves, with his eyes glowing,
About the places he plans on going.

Of course, he probably finds it hard
(Forever circling his liquid yard)
To know the spot where his trips begin
And whether he's going or he's been.

But even when told Which Way Is West,
A goldfish still doesn't seem impressed.

You tell a goldfish the time of day
Or what he's having for dinner, say,
Or what the weather prediction is,
and see if you get a glad "Gee whiz!"

You're lucky to get, for all your trouble,
A passing comment of one small bubble.

Share:

Sharp, N. L. *Today I'm Going Fishing with My Dad.* Art by Chris L. Demarest. Boyds
    Mill, 1993.

    A little boy hates to go fishing, but enjoys the outing with his dad.

Wilcox, Cathy. *Enzo the Wonderfish.* Art by the author. Ticknor, 1994.

    A little boy tries to teach his pet goldfish tricks.

BIRDSEED

Awakening

by Geoffrey Summerfield

Leave this bird-seed
To sleep in the seed-bed,
And see the sparrows
Sprout next Spring.

Valentines

by Aileen Fisher

I gave a hundred Valentines.
A hundred, did I say?
I gave a *thousand* Valentines
one cold and wintry day.

I didn't put my name on them
or any other words,
because my Valentines were seeds
for February birds.

Pass out small, resealable bags of birdseed.

SPELLING

Spelling Bee

by Cynthia Rylant

Best speller since third grade
that Beaver Elementary
had ever seen.
Could spell *assassination*
when I was nine.
When I was eleven
entered the
Big Spelling Bee.
Winning would mean
a try at the
county championship
and then—the world.
Everyone knew I'd win.
But first, I had to
win at Beaver.
Nervous beyond words,
I was asked to spell
woke.
Sputtered W-O-A-K.
WOAK.
Knew I'd blown it,
just nervous,
but made them check a
dictionary, anyway,
to save myself some
dignity
and on the chance that
some stupid idiot
like me

175

had used it in a
spelling bee
and made it
a word.
It wasn't.

People There

by Byrd Baylor

People there
did things
in their own way.
For instance—
spelling.

Sometimes I'd be
surprised
at how my father
spelled a word
that I'd already learned
at school,
but if I mentioned it,
he'd say,
"The way I spell it
is the way
they spelled it
there,
so it must be right.

But my mother said
since we weren't living
there,

maybe we should just
go ahead
and spell the way
they do in other places.
So we did,
though we always liked
his way.

Maybe that's part of the reason
it was the best town
in the world.
You could do things
whatever way
seemed good
to you.

Hold your own spelling bee and honor the winner and the losers. These poems would also complement a longer, themed program on words and language (see chapter 13).

ONIONS

Why Do Onions Make Us Cry?

by Amy Goldman Koss

Why do onions make us cry?
Tomatoes do not make us cry
　　But onions surely do.
Why do onions bring on tears,
　　And make us go "boohoo"?

When we cut an onion,
We break apart its cells.
Inside the cell is onion oil
Which really, really smells!

The oil turns to vapors
That sting our nose and eyes.
To wash away the stinging stuff,
The eye makes tears and cries!

The Wind Is Like an Onion

by Liz Rosenberg

The wind is like an onion.
It wears seven layers,
hides in a sack,
makes your eyes water.
And when you bite into it
it bites back.

This last poem is about wind, not an onion, but the two poems make a good contrast of images, similes, and metaphors.

Supermarket

by Felice Holman

I'm
lost
among a
maze of cans,
behind a pyramid
of jams, quite near
asparagus and rice,
close to the Oriental spice,
and just before sardines.
I hear my mother calling, "Joe.
Where are you, Joe? Where did you
Go?" And I reply in voice concealed among
the candied orange peel, and packs of Chocolate Dreams.

"I
hear
you, Mother
dear, I'm here—
quite near the ginger ale
and beer, and lost among a
                maze
            of cans
          behind a
        pyramid of jams,
      quite near asparagus
    and rice, close to the
Oriental spice, and just before sardines."

But
still
my mother
calls me, "Joe?
Where are you, Joe?
Where did you go?"

"Somewhere
around asparagus
that's in a sort of
broken glass,
beside a kind of m-
ess-
y jell
that's near a tower of cans that f
e
l
l
and squashed the Chocolate Dreams."

MARKETS

Jamaica Market

by Agnes Maxwell-Hall

Honey, pepper, leaf-green limes
Pagan fruit whose names are rhymes,
Mangoes, breadfruit, ginger-roots,
Granadillas, bamboo shoots.
Cho-cho, ackees, tangerines,
Lemons, purple Congo-beans,
Sugar, okras, kola-nuts,
Citrons, hairy cocoanuts,
Fish, tobacco, native hats,
Gold bananas, woven mats,
Plantains, wild-thyme, pallid leeks,
Pigeons with their scarlet beaks,
Oranges and saffron yams,
Baskets, ruby guava jams,
Turtles, goat-skins, cinnamon,
Allspice, conch-shells, golden rum.
Black skins, babel—and the sun
That burns all colors into one.

Most children in the United States are not familiar with the open markets prevalent in so many other countries, but they should be able to feel the rhythm, color, and exotic flavor of this poem. On the other hand, almost all have been in an American supermarket and will relate to this adventure.

Share:
Hautzig, David. *At the Supermarket.* Photos by author. Orchard, 1994.
Lessac, Frané. *Caribbean Canvas.* Boyds Mill, 1994.

SQUIRRELS

Squirrel

by Felice Holman

Scolding
Holding
Boldly raiding
Plotting
Waiting
Ambuscading
Highly climbing
And descending
Digging
Hiding
And forgetting.

Squirrel

by Yoshiko Uchida

Hey, squirrel
Munching
Crunching
On that hickory nut.

I used to
Like you
Until I learned
You're just a
Rodent
With a bushy tail.

Padiddle

by J. Patrick Lewis

"They must be here *some*where
    Said Mrs. McPotts
Whose dizzy Dalmatian
    Was missing his spots.

"You *had* them at breakfast,
    You wore them outside!
Now where could one hundred
    And twenty spots hide?"

She ransacked the attic,
    She rummaged through drawers,
She ripped the linoleum
    Tile from the floors!

"Padiddle!" she shouted
    (For that was his name),
"I've never played such
    A ridiculous game!"

And that's when it happened,
    Poor Mrs. McPotts
Snuck a peek in the mirror—
    At Mrs. McSpotts!

My Uncle Charlie

by Valerie Osborne

I have an uncle,
Charlie Bloggs,
Who's very fond
Of spotted dogs.
He goes around
In London fogs,
Painting spots
On plain black dogs.

The presenters could be dressed in polka dots and you might consider an art project involving lots of spots.

Share:

Harshman, Marc. *Uncle James*. Art by Michael Dooling. Cobblehill, 1993.

Jimmy is disappointed that Uncle James is not the hero he had expected. This makes a nice discussion-starter.

Gleeson, Libby. *Uncle David*. Art by Armin Greder. Tambourine, 1992.

Ned, the smallest person in the class brags about his giant uncle.

Zucker, David. *Uncle Carmello*. Art by Lyle Miller. Macmillan, 1993.

David learns to respect his uncle.

Homework

by Russell Hoban

Homework sits on top of Sunday, squashing Sunday flat.
Homework has the smell of Monday, homework's very fat.
Heavy books and piles of paper, answers I don't know.
Sunday evening's almost finished, now I'm going to go
Do my homework in the kitchen. Maybe just a snack,
Then I'll sit right down and start as soon as I run back
For some chocolate sandwich cookies. Then I'll really do
All that homework in a minute. First I'll see what new
Show they've got on television in the living room.
Everybody's laughing there, but misery and gloom
And a full refrigerator are where I am at.
I'll just have another sandwich. Homework's very fat.

Homework

by Jane Yolen

What is it about homework
That makes me want to write
My Great Aunt Myrt to thank her for
The sweater that's too tight?

What is it about homework
That makes me pick up socks
That stink from days and days of wear.
Then clean the litter box?

What is it about homework
That makes me volunteer
To take the garbage out before
The bugs and flies appear?

What is it about homework
That makes me wash my hair
And take an hour combing out
The snags and tangles there?

What is it about homework?
You know, I wish I knew.
'Cause nights when I've got homework
I've got too much to do!

These two poems can either be presented in a straightforward manner, letting the audience identify the familiar conflict, or the presenters can mime the actions that compete with homework for their attention.

SPORTS

Overdog

by Tony Johnston

Overdog Johnson is a guy
who always wins
but hardly tries.

Pitcher sails it.
Johnson nails it.
Whack!
Homerun!

Pitcher steams it.
Johnson creams it.
Thwack!
Homerun!

Pitcher smokes it.
Johnson pokes it.
Smack!
Homerun!

Pitcher fires it.
Johnson wires it.
Crack!
Ho-hum.

Foul Shot

by Edwin A. Hoey

With two 60's stuck on the scoreboard
And two seconds hanging on the clock,
The solemn boy in the center of eyes,
Squeezed by silence,
Seeks out the line with his feet,
Soothes his hands along his uniform,
Gently drums the ball against the floor
Then measures the waiting net,
Raises the ball on his right hand,
Balances it with his left,
Calms it with fingertips,
Breathes,
Crouches,
Waits,
And then through a stretching of stillness,
Nudges it upward.

The ball slides up and out,
Lands,
Leans,
Wobbles,
Wavers,
Hesitates,
Exasperates,

Plays it coy
Until every face begs with unsounding screams,
And then,

        And then

            And then,

    Right before ROAR-UP,
Dives down and through.

Consider having one presenter carry a bat and ball, the other a basketball. They may want to wear sports uniforms as costumes.

13

Theme Poetry

You may have already tried "partnered" or mini-theme poems with the same or related subjects. Now, you may want to offer a slightly more ambitious poetry break as a program for your own class, the school, or the community.

One way of doing this is to choose your favorite poems from throughout the book and present them as a potpourri. You can alternate short and long poems, serious and humorous poems. The program will still not take a lot of time from your meeting or class time. This is yet another option for introducing more poems and using more presenters. By the time you are ready to do this kind of program, you probably will have some eager volunteers who want their turn to do the poetry break.

Another way of doing a program is to find poems that relate to a particular subject or theme. The poems in this chapter are arranged in this way, but all need not be used together. For example, you may want to present just one birthday poem to celebrate someone's birthday and on another occasion use all the selections at a birthday party or assembly honoring all the children with birthdays during a particular month.

Perhaps you would like to celebrate one particular theme for an entire week of poetry breaks. Call it an animal or weather week and present a poem every day on the same subject.

FAMILY AND NEIGHBORS

Children may want to dress up as the people represented in these poems, or exhibit portraits they've drawn of their own special people, or how they imagine the characters in the poem would look.

FAMILY AND NEIGHBORS POEMS

remembering . . . • Nikki Grimes

The Sugar Lady • Frank Asch

Hot Line • Louella Dunann

Missing Mama • Eloise Greenfield

Zeroing in • Diane Dawber

Look Up! • Ann Turner

Borders • Arnold Adoff

They were my people • Grace Nichols

remembering . . .

by Nikki Grimes

remembering
Grandma filling up this porch
with laughing
and stories about when
Mama was a little girl
and Grandma would hug me
and say
I was her very special own granddaughter.
But now she's gone.
I miss her—

The Sugar Lady

by Frank Asch

There is an old lady who lives down the hall,
Wrinkled and gray and toothless and small.
At seven already she's up,
Going from door to door with a cup.
"Do you have any sugar?" she asks,
Although she's got more than you.
"Do you have any sugar?" she asks,
Hoping you'll talk for a minute or two.

Hot Line

by Louella Dunann

Our daughter, Alicia,
Had just turned sixteen,
And was earning the title
Of "Telephone Queen."

For her birthday we gave her
Her own private phone
Along with instructions
To leave ours alone.

Now we still catch her using
Our line, with the stall,
"I can't tie mine up, Mom,
I might get a call."

194

Missing Mama

by Eloise Greenfield

last year when Mama died
I went to my room to hide
from the hurt
I closed my door
wasn't going to come out
no more, never
but my uncle he said
you going to get past
this pain
      you going to
push on past this pain
and one of these days
you going to feel like
yourself again
I don't miss a day
remembering Mama
sometimes I cry
but mostly
I think about
the good things
now

Zeroing in

by Diane Dawber

The tree down the street
  has little green apples
    that never get bigger
      never turn red.
They just drop on the ground
  get worm holes
    brown spots.
They're
  just right for stepping on
    like walking on bumpy marbles,
      or green eggs that break with a snap
        just right for gathering
          in a heap behind the hedge
          waiting
            for a target.
Here comes my brother.

Look Up!

by Ann Turner

Do you ever see
how grown-ups don't look up
when they walk? They stare
at their feet,
the store windows,
some car they're mad at.

One day the taxi drivers
beeped and yelled,
people charged up the street
and I saw above
this huge gray bird
sailing along like we were the sea
and he looked for an island
to land on.

No one saw him,
no one but me and one
old lady who yelled, "Look,
everybody, look! A great blue
heron in New York!" I don't know
about no blue heron, but I do know
grown-ups need to look up
more.

Borders

by Arnold Adoff

Great Grandma Ida came from a small village
in Poland
      on the Russian border
      to America,
      on a ship that   sailed
      for weeks,
      on the rough Atlantic
             Ocean:

to make a new place for her self;
to work in a factory; to find her father;
to find a man
      from a German town on the Polish
               border
to marry; to have and raise a daughter
      who would find and marry
      a man from a Russian town
             on the Polish
             border.

And in 1935 they would have a baby boy
      in a New York City hospital
Who is daddy now to
      me.

198

They Were My People

by Grace Nichols

They were those who cut cane
to the rhythm of the sunbeat

They were those who carried cane
to the rhythm of the sunbeat

They were those who crushed cane
to the rhythm of the sunbeat

They were women weeding, carrying babies
to the rhythm of the sunbeat

They were my people, working so hard
to the rhythm of the sunbeat—long ago
to the rhythm of the sunbeat

BIRTHDAYS

Celebrating a birthday? Use one or more of these poems to help celebrate. Exhibit birthday books or books on a subject or theme that the birthday boy or girl enjoys reading.

BIRTHDAY POEMS:

Birthdays • Marchette Chute

What someone said when he was spanked on the day before his birthday • John Ciardi

Birthdays • Mary Ann Hoberman

Happy Birthday Card • Rony Robinson

Between Birthdays • Ogden Nash

Birthday Weather • Siv Widerberg

Happy Birthday, Dear Dragon • Jack Prelutsky

In the Cupboard • Barbara Ireson

Birthdays

by Marchette Chute

We had waffles-with-syrup for breakfast
    As many as we could hold;
And I had some presents extra,
    Because I am nine years old.

I've thanked everyone for my presents,
    And kissed 'em, and now that that's done
The family's all ready to do things,
    Whatever I think would be fun.

When Timothy had his birthday
    We went to the circus, and Tim
Made friends with the seals and the monkeys
    And a real clown winked at him.

And Dorothy chose a picnic
    On the shore of a little lake,
With tadpoles, and buns, and diving,
    And a four-layer birthday cake.

And now that it's my turn for choosing,
    I'm going to ask if we might
Take all of our family of rabbits
    To bed with us just for tonight.

What someone said when he was spanked on the day before his birthday

by John Ciardi

Some day
I may
Pack my bag and run away.
Some day
I may.
—But not today.

Some night
I might
Slip away in the moonlight.
I might.
Some night.
—But not tonight.

Some night.
Some day.
I might.
I may.
—But right now I think I'll stay.

Birthdays

by Mary Ann Hoberman

If birthdays happened once a week
Instead of once a year,
Think of all the gifts you'd get
And all the songs you'd hear
And think of how quickly you'd grow up;
Wouldn't it feel queer
If birthdays happened once a week
Instead of once a year?

Happy Birthday Card

by Rony Robinson

H   appy birthday all of us say
A   nd may you have a lovely day.
P   lenty of nice dreams!
P   resents and ice creams!
Y   ucky buns!
B   est of fun!
I   nteresting invitations!
R   ailway stations!
T   elly and trips!
H   amburgers and chips! BUT
D   o get a cough (if)
A   nd I hope your knees fall off (if)
Y   ou forget mine

Between Birthdays

by Ogden Nash

My birthdays take so long to start.
They come along a year apart.
It's worse than waiting for a bus;
I fear I used to fret and fuss,
But now, when by impatience vexed
Between one birthday and the next,
I think of all that I have seen
That keeps on happening in between.
The songs I've heard, the things I've done,
Make my un-birthdays not so un-

Birthday Weather

by Siv Widerberg

Sunny
or rainy
or only a little sunny
or the brightest sunniest day of the year
Tomorrow
the third of June
is my birthday

But then of course
if it were sunny
on Everyone's birthday
it Never would rain

But tomorrow
the third of June
is My Birthday

Happy Birthday, Dear Dragon

by Jack Prelutsky

There were rumblings of strange jubilation
in a dark, subterranean lair,
for the dragon was having a birthday,
and his colleagues were gathering there.
"HOORAH!" groaned the trolls and the ogres
as they pelted each other with stones.
"HOORAH!" shrieked a sphinx and a griffin,
and the skeletons rattled their bones.

"*HOORAH!*" screamed the queen of the demons,
"HOORAH!" boomed a giant. **"REJOICE!"**

"hoorah!" piped a tiny hobgoblin
in an almost inaudible voice.
"HOORAH!" cackled rapturous witches,
"*Hoorahhhhhh!*" hissed a basilisk too.
Then they howled in cacophonous chorus,
"HAPPY BIRTHDAY,
    DEAR DRAGON,
      TO YOU!"

They whistled, they squawked, they applauded,
as they gleefully brought forth the cake.
"OH, THANK YOU!"
he thundered with pleasure
in a bass that made every ear ache.
Then puffing his chest to the fullest,
and taking deliberate aim,
the dragon huffed once at the candles—

and
the candles
all burst
into
flame!

207

In the Cupboard

by Barbara Ireson

I went to the cupboard
And what did I see?
One lemon
Two oranges
Three apples
Four pears
Five peaches
Six plums
Seven bananas
Eight cherries
Nine gooseberries
Ten raspberries
And up on a shelf
All by itself
A birthday cake for me.

TIMES OF THE YEAR

These poems can be used individually to accompany the appropriate weather, season, or holiday—or use any of them in more general programs on these topics. For a fresh look at a seasonal celebration or phenomenon, recite them out of calendar sequence. They are presented here as a grab bag, not a month by month culling, so you can mix and match in surprising ways.

You can share these books any time you present weather poems as a poetry break:

Harvey, Amanda. *Stormy Weather*. Lothrop, 1992.
Lotz, Karen E. *Can't Sit Still*. Art by Colleen Browning. Dutton, 1993.

A young girl exhuberantly enjoys the seasons in the city.
Simon, Seymour. *Weather*. Illustrated with photographs. Morrow, 1993.

Large format picture book explores the phenomenon of weather.

TIMES OF THE YEAR POEMS:

Burglar • Deborah Chandra

The muddy puddle • Dennis Lee

Rhyme of Rain • John Holmes

December • Sanderson Vanderbilt

Something Told the Wild Geese • Rachel Field

Daffodils • William Wordsworth

Moon of Falling Leaves (Collected from the Cherokee) • Joseph Bruchac and Jonathan London

The Summer Storm • Rebecca Caudill

The Poetry Break

Seaside • Shirley Hughes

in Just-spring • e.e. cummings

April Rain Song • Langston Hughes

Wake Up • Zaro Weil

Wild Day at the Shore • Felice Holman

Windstorm in Brooklyn • Tony Johnston

Knoxville, Tennessee • Nikki Giovanni

September Is • Bobbi Katz

Arbor Day • Marchette Chute

Court Jester's Last Report to the King • Jack Prelutsky

Thanksgiving Mouse • Grace Tall

Conversation Hearts • Nina Payne

Christmas morning i • Carol Freeman

Wearing of the Green • Aileen Fisher

Fourth of July • Barbara Juster Esbensen

The Pony on Halloween • Patricia Hubbell

One Day Only • Marchette Chute

Burglar

by Deborah Chandra

Rain
Creeps
Upon my rooftop
Like a burglar
In the night,
Runs fingers
Round my windows,
Finding everything
Shut tight.
Startled
when the morning dawns,
it dangles from the eaves,
Drops d
      o
       w
        n,
Sneaking away
Without a sound,
Leaving small
Footprints
on
the
Ground.

The muddy puddle

by Dennis Lee

I am sitting
in the middle
of a rather Muddy
Puddle.
With my bottom
Full of bubbles
And my rubbers
Full of Mud,

While my jacket
And my sweater
Go on slowly
Getting wetter
As I very
Slowly settle
To the Bottom
Of the Mud.

And I find that
What a person
With a puddle
Round his middle
Thinks of mostly
In the muddle
Is the Muddi-
Ness of Mud.

Rhyme of Rain

by John Holmes

"Fifty stories more to fall,
Nothing in our way at all,"
Said a raindrop to its mate
Falling near the Empire State.
Said the second, "Here we go!
That's Fifth Avenue below."
Said the first one, "There's a hat.
Watch me land myself on that.
Forty stories isn't far—
Thirty-seven—here we are—
Twenty, sixteen, thirteen, ten—"
"If we make this trip again,"
Said the second, "we must fall
Near a building twice as tall."
"What a time to think of that,"
Said the first, and missed the hat.

December

by Sanderson Vanderbilt

A little boy stood on the corner
And shoveled bits of dirty, soggy snow
Into the sewer—
With a jagged piece of tin.

He was helping spring come.

Something Told the Wild Geese

by Rachel Field

Something told the wild geese
It was time to go.
Though the fields lay golden
something whispered—"snow."
Leaves were green and stirring,
Berries, luster-glossed,
But beneath warm feathers
something cautioned—"frost."
All the sagging orchards
Steamed with amber spice,
But each wild beast stiffened
at remembered ice.
Something told the wild geese
It was time to fly—
Summer sun was on their wings,
Winter in their cry.

Daffodils

by William Wordsworth

I wandered lonely as a cloud
that floats on high o'er vales and hills,
when all at once I saw a crowd,
a host, of golden daffodils;
beside the lake, beneath the trees,
fluttering and dancing in the breeze.

Moon of Falling Leaves

Collected from the Cherokee
by Joseph Bruschac
and Jonathan London

Long ago, the trees were told
they must stay awake
seven days and nights,
but only the cedar,
the pine and the spruce
stayed awake until
that seventh night.
The reward they were given
was to always be green,
while all the other trees
must shed their leaves.

So, each autumn, the leaves
of the sleeping trees fall.
They cover the floor
of our woodlands with colors
as bright as the flowers
that come with the spring.
The leaves return the strength
of one more year's growth
to the earth.

This journey
the leaves are taking
is part of the great circle
which holds us all close to the earth.

The Summer Storm

by Rebecca Caudill

The summer storm comes
   Bolting white lightning; it goes
      Muttering thunder.

Seaside

by Shirley Hughes

Sand in the sandwiches,
Sand in the tea,
Flat, wet sand running
Down to the sea.
Pools full of seaweed,
Shells and stones,
Damp bathing suits
And ice-cream cones.
Waves pouring in
To a sand-castle moat.
Mend the defences!
Now we're afloat!
Water's for splashing,
Sand is for play,
A day by the sea
Is the best kind of day.

in Just–spring

by e. e. cummings

in Just-
spring   when the world is mud-
luscious and the little
lame balloonman

whistles   far   and wee

and eddieandbill come
running from marbles and
piracies and it's
spring

when the world is puddle-wonderful

the queer
old balloonman whistles
far   and   wee
and bettyandisbel come dancing

from hopscotch and jump-rope and
it's
spring
and
    the

        goat-footed
balloonman   whistles
far
and
wee

April Rain Song

by Langston Hughes

Let the rain kiss you.
Let the rain beat upon your head with silver liquid drops.
Let the rain sing you a lullaby.

The rain makes still pools on the sidewalk.
The rain makes running pools in the gutter.
The rain plays a little sleep-song on our roof at night—

And I love the rain.

Wake Up

by Zaro Weil

Wake up

Morning
Has
Galloped
Bareback
All night to
Get here

Wild Day at the Shore

by Felice Holman

Upward a gull
Outward a tern
Upward and outward and seaward.
Inward the wind
Downward the waves
Inward and downward and leeward.
    Wind, waves, and sky.
    Gull, tern, and I.

Windstorm in Brooklyn

by Tony Johnston

Brooklyn was swept by a
windstorm one day.
Afghans and poodles were
carried away.
Children slurped cereal,
soaring aloft.
Some of them bumped into
clouds (pillow-soft).
Ladies with teacups sipped
tea on the fly.
Criss-crossing neighbors yelled,
"Hi!" in the sky.
Most of the city was
tossed in the air—
except for the birds, which were
already there.

Knoxville, Tennessee

by Nikki Giovanni

I always like summer
best
you can eat fresh corn
from daddy's garden
and okra
and greens
and cabbage
and lots of
barbecue
and buttermilk
and homemade ice-cream
at the church picnic
and listen to
gospel music
outside
at the church
homecoming
and go to the mountains with
your grandmother
and go barefooted
and be warm
all the time
not only when you go to bed
and sleep

September Is

by Bobbi Katz

September is
when yellow pencils
in brand new eraser hats
bravely wait on perfect points—
ready to march across miles of lines
in empty notebooks—
and
September is
when a piece of chalk
skates across the board—
swirling and looping—
until it spells your new teacher's
name.

Arbor Day

by Marchette Chute

Today in school we planted a tree
    And all of us knew just how
to cover its roots most carefully.
    It's only a baby now,

But every year it will grow and grow
    For everyone to see,
And after a while, as all of us know,
    It will be a grown-up tree.

The Court Jester's Last Report to the King

by Jack Prelutsky

Oh sire! My Sire! your castle's on fire,
I fear it's about to explode,
a hideous lizard has eaten the wizard,
the prince has turned into a toad.

Oh sire! Good sire! there's woe in the shire,
fierce trolls are arriving in force,
there are pirates in port, monstrous ogres at court,
and a dragon has melted your horse.

Oh sire! Great sire! the tidings are dire,
a giant has trampled the school,
your army has fled, there are bees in your bed
and your nose has come off . . . APRIL FOOL!

The Thanksgiving Mouse

by Grace Cornell Tall

Once, uninvited to my house,
A stranger-mouse slipped in;
He spied an open cider-pail
And, curious, fell in—
Unluckily, when he was young
He never learned to swim
(And there I was with fourteen guests
And no spare chair for him!)
This happened on Thanksgiving Day,
And no one gave thanks more
Than this mouse did when, by his tail,
I plucked him from the cider-pail
And showed him to the door,
But not before I stuffed his vest
With the sugar cookies he liked best
To cheer him on his way.
And that is how a stranger-mouse,
Though uninvited to my house,
Enjoyed Thanksgiving Day.

Conversation Hearts

by Nina Payne

In February, bring them home,
pink, yellow, lavender
and lime pastels
BE MINE   I'M YOURS
to be read by the tongue
that licks the chalk
and tastes what it spells.

I'll give you a boxful,
tasting of daphne, lupin,
mint and columbine;
a mouthful of secrets,
lovelier than whispers,
dear ones, friends
I'M YOURS   BE MINE

For a souvenir-treat distribute conversation heart candies.

Share:

Modell, Frank. *One Million Valentines*. Art by the author. Greenwillow, 1981.

Marvin and Milton make and deliver valentines to all the people in the neighborhood.

Christmas morning i

by Carol Freeman

Christmas morning i
got up before the others and
ran
naked across the plank
floor into the front
room to see grandmama
sewing a new
button on my last year
ragdoll.

Wearing of the Green

by Aileen Fisher

It ought to come in April
or, better yet, in May
when everything is green as green—
I mean St. Patrick's Day.

With still a week of winter
this wearing of the green
seems rather out of season—
it's rushing things, I mean.

But maybe March *is* better
when all is done and said:
St. Patrick brings a promise,
a four-leaf-clover promise,
a green-all-over promise
of springtime just ahead!

226

Fourth of July

by Barbara Juster Esbensen

Tonight the air explodes!
Sparkling fragments burn
and scatter.   Fire cascades
falls   pours into the dark
like water.

Dazzled by bomb-burst
we lift our faces
to the spangled sky.   We are
fire-worshippers. Our one long breath
is AHHHHHHHHH
and OHHHHHHHHHH.   Our eyes reflect
the blazine seeds
that drift on the wind
and sputter out.

Walking home
we have the cold stars
and fireflies
tangled in the grass.

The Pony on Halloween

by Patricia Hubbell

A Shetland pony,
dark brown
and in full winter coat,
escaped from his paddock
one Halloween
and wandered
into town.
Sending running:
   Three witches,
   one goblin,
   two clowns,
   and a truck driver
   from Canada,
   who hurriedly
   climbed into his cab,
   shouting:
      "Bear! Bear! Bear!"
Upon which,
the Shetland
trotted back
to his pen
and smugly whinnied:
      "I may be Woolly and Small—
      But I tricked them All!"

One Day Only

by Marchette Chute

I answered back today in school.
I put a frog in the swimming pool.
I stole a cake that was left to cool.
No, I didn't.
    April Fool!

ANIMALS

For an unusual grouping on a familiar theme, try presenting some of these sightly offbeat observations on the animal kingdom.

ANIMAL THEME POEMS:

Pigeons • Marchette Chute

The Dog • Jeanne Steig

Chums • Arthur Guiterman

The first horses were made of sea foam • David Day

Mosquitoes • Jean Little

The Goat • Anonymous

The Turkey • John Gardner

Giraffe • William Jay Smith

Pigeons

by Marchette Chute

Pigeons do
   Annoy me so.
I creep behind them
   Nice and slow.
They do not care
   How close I get.

I haven't caught
   A pigeon yet.

The Dog

by Jeanne Steig

Which pet is most beloved by man?
The cat? The horse? The ortolan?
The chimpanzee? The winsome hog?
Not on your life! It is the dog.

At certain tasks the dog excels,
Like pulling babies out of wells
And finding travelers in the snow
And fetching things that people throw.

What energy the dog expends
In welcoming your foes and friends!
A noble beast when at his best!
At other times, alas, a pest.

Chums

by Arthur Guiterman

He sits and begs, he gives a paw.
He is, as you can see,
The finest dog you ever saw,
And he belongs to me.

He follows everywhere I go
And even when I swim.
I laugh because he thinks, you know,
That I belong to him.

But still, no matter what we do
We never have a fuss;
And so, I guess, it must be true
That *we* belong to *us*.

The first horses were made of sea foam

by David Day

The first horses were made of sea foam.

They rode their waves to the beaches
Then broke loose and dashed for the shore.

Wild horses, raging with pride—
Look how much of the untamed sea

Is within them still.

Mosquitoes

by Jean Little

I came in just in time for supper
But there wasn't any.
Mother was lying on the couch with her eyes shut.
"Mother," I said, "What are you doing?"
I thought she wasn't going to answer.
She didn't open her eyes.
But, after a minute, she said,
"Use your powers of observation, Kate.
Obviously I am leading the animals into the Ark
—two by two."
"What do you want for supper," I asked.
. . . Silence . . .
"Mother," I began again.
"Don't interrupt me," she murmured from far away,
"Or I might forget mosquitoes."

So I made Kraft dinner and a salad.
When I took her plate in to her, she had fallen asleep.
She comes home from work terribly tired some nights.
I put her macaroni in the oven and her salad in the refrigerator.
Then, right in the middle of doing French, I thought,
"Maybe we won't have any mosquitoes this summer."
I laughed out loud and wakened her.
"What's so funny?" she yawned.
"Never mind," I said. I got her her supper.
She didn't make me explain.
Maybe she knew
That saying one word more would have spoiled it.

The Goat

Anonymous

There was a man, now please take note,
There was a man, who had a goat,
He lov'd that goat, indeed he did,
He lov'd that goat, just like a kid.

One day that goat felt frisk and fine,
Ate three red shirts from off the line.
The man he grabbed him by the back,
And tied him to the railroad track.

But when the train hove into sight,
That goat grew pale and green with fright.
He heaved a sigh, as if in pain,
Coughed up those shirts and flagged the train.

The Turkey

by John Gardner

The Turkey's so dumb he can drown in the rain;
Revive the poor creature, he'll do it again.

He wouldn't approve of Thanksgiving, no doubt;
If the Turkey was able to figure it out.

But he doesn't think twice, he just eats and gets fat
And along comes the axman and, well sir, that's that.

We needn't feel guilty or sniffle or wince;
If it wasn't for us, he'd have died out long since.

It's Man's tender care that makes Turkeys thrive;
If we'd eaten the dodo he'd still be alive.

Giraffe

by William Jay Smith

When I invite the Giraffe to dine,
I ask a carpenter friend of mine
To build a table so very tall
It takes up nearly the whole front hall.
The Giraffe and I do not need chairs:
He stands—I sit on the top of the stairs;
And we eat from crisp white paper plates
A meal of bananas, figs, and dates.

He whispers, when the table's clear,
Just loud enough for me to hear:
"Come one day soon to dine with me
And sit high up in a banyan tree
While Beasts of earth and sea and air
Gather all around us there,
All around the Unicorn
Who leads them with his lowered horn—

And we'll eat *without* white paper plates
A meal of bananas, figs, and dates."

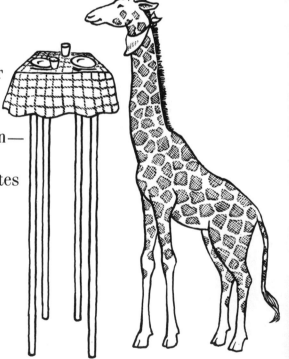

236

WORDS AND BOOKS

Be sure to offer a selection of books on exhibit with this theme. And think about bringing your dictionary and sharing a few intriguing words with your group. Some books to share might include:

Aliki. *How a Book Is Made.* Art by the author. Harper, 1986.

　　Surveys the bookmaking process in cartoons.

Brillhort, Julie. *Story Hour—Starring Megan!* Art by the author. Whitman, 1992.

　　When her mother the librarian is busy, Megan puts on the story hour.

WORDS AND BOOKS POEMS:

I Want to Lock Out the World • Michele Krueger

A stubby • Bonnie Larkin Nims

The Alphabet Monster • Robert Heidbreder

Condensed Version • Jean Little

Fish • Ivor Cutler

The Fly • Charlotte Zolotow

A Remarkable Adventure • Jack Prelutsky

Books on the Prowl! • Rick Kilcup

Read to me Riddles • Jane Yolen

Pencils • Barbara Juster Esbensen

The Poetry Break

The Library Cheer • Garrison Keilor.

Book Lice • Paul Fleischman

Sam at the Library • Carol Combs Hole

Reading is Dangerous • Tony Johnston

I Want to Lock Out the World

by Michele Krueger

I want to lock out the world
and barricade it,
ceiling to floor.
I found a treasure,
an unspeakable pleasure,
a book I've not read before!

A stubby

by Bonnie Larkin Nims

A stubby,
rubbery
tip of a tongue
licks up
letters and numbers
I got wrong,
makes my paper
look like new.

(I wish it could tell me
the right answer, too!)

?

{The answer to this riddle-poem is, of course, an eraser—but let the children guess it.}

The Alphabet Monster

by Robert Heidbreder

I'm the Alphabet Monster
And nothing tastes better
To the Alphabet Monster
Than eating a letter.
A "j" and an "a"
And a "c" and a "k"
And the million more letters
I munch every day.

I'm hungry now.
What shall I do?
I think I'll eat
a "y"
an "o"
and a "u".

That means . . . YOU!

240

Condensed Version

by Jean Little

When I went to the Blairs',
Emily was reading her cousin Ann a condensed version
   of *Heidi*.
It was all wrong—the pictures, the words,
     what happened, the way it felt.
"You shouldn't read her that," I said.
"Why not?" asked Emily.
Suddenly, I knew how to explain.
"People who read condensed versions instead of the real book," I
   said loftily,
"Are like people who read a road map
      —and think they've been on a journey."
Emily looked at me, for a moment.
Then she put down the book and clapped.

"*Read*, Emily!" Ann said.
"Let's read *Winnie-the-Pooh* instead," said Emily.

I stayed to listen.
It was the one about Eeyore's birthday.
We liked it as much as Ann.

How perfect of Emily to clap like that!

Fish

by Ivor Cutler

Fish
are not
very bright
not
by my
standards.
They
never had any
reason to grow
brains. For
one thing
it's hard
to read
under water and
the paper gets too wet
to handle and
there isn't the light and
fins let books slip and you'd
have to hold the
pen in your mouth.

People
who say
'A school of fish'
are
taking
advantage of

their limited
intelligence to poke cruel
fun.

You let
fish be.

Or eat them.

The Fly

by Charlotte Zolotow

I was sitting on the porch
reading my book
in the summer sun.

A fly
settled on my page
black as ink.

Quivering and alive,
rubbing one leg against the other,
he sat on a word.

Share:
Peters, Lisa Westberg. When the fly flew in . . . . Art by Brad Sneed. Dial, 1994.

A Remarkable Adventure

by Jack Prelutsky

I was at my bedroom table
with a notebook open wide,
when a giant anaconda
started winding up my side,
I was filled with apprehension
and retreated down the stairs,
to be greeted at the bottom
by a dozen grizzly bears.

We tumultuously tussled
till I managed to get free,
then I saw, with trepidation,
there were tigers after me,
I could feel them growing closer,
I was quivering with fear,
then I blundered into quicksand
and began to disappear.

I was rescued by an eagle
that descended from the skies
to embrace me with its talons,
to my terror and surprise,
but that raptor lost its purchase
when a blizzard made me sneeze,
and it dropped me in a thicket
where I battered both my knees.

I was suddenly surrounded
by a troop of savage trolls,

who maliciously informed me
they would toast me over coals,
I was lucky to elude them
when they briefly looked away—
that's the reason why my homework
isn't here with me today.

Books on the Prowl!

by Rick Kilcup

Books are on the prowl, the prowl!
Books are on the prowl!
Full of lions
tigers
dragons
and the
wolf's spine-chilling howl.

Books are on the prowl, the prowl!
Out to suck you in!
Full of mysteries
fairies
giants
and the
ogre's wicked grin!

Books are on the prowl, the prowl!
Set to cast their spell!
Full of pirates
spaceships
heroes
with their
stories there to tell.

Books are on the prowl, the prowl!
So here's what you must do!
Grab 'em! Hug 'em! Read 'em . . .
before they can pounce on you!

Read to Me Riddles

by Jane Yolen

Read to me riddles
and read to me rhymes,
read to me stories
of magical times.

Read to me tales
about castles and kings,
read to me stories
of fabulous things.

Read to me pirates,
and read to me knights,
read to me dragons
and dragon-back flights.

Read to me spaceships
and cowboys and then
when you are finished—
please read them again!

Pencils

by Barbara Juster Esbensen

The rooms in a pencil
are narrow
but elephants   castles and watermelons
fit in

In a pencil
noisy words yell for attention
and quiet words wait their turn

How did they slip
into such a tight place?
Who
gives them their
lunch?

From a broken pencil
an unbroken poem will come!
There is a long story living
in the shortest pencil

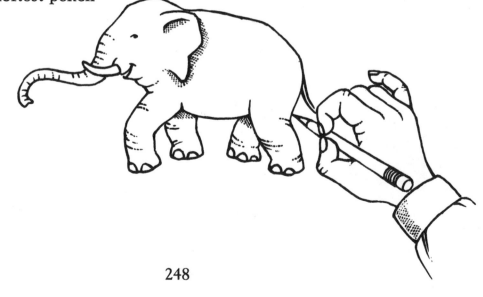

The Library Cheer

by Garrison Keillor

Where do you go for the poetry?
L-I-B-R-A-R-Y
Where do you go for the history?
L-I-B-R-A-R-Y
Where do you go if you're old and shy?
Where do you go to learn how to fly?
L-I-B-R-A-R-Y
    That's how you spell it,
    Whatcha gonna tell it?
It's been in your town for a hundred years.
Let's give the library three big cheers:
    Hip-hip-hooray!
    Hip-hip-hooray!
    Hip-hip-hooray!
F-R-I-E-N-D-S
Are we gonna be one?
Yes yes yes.
F-R-I-E-N-D-S
Are we gonna be one?
Yes yes yes.
F-R-I-E-N-D-S (of the)
P-U-B-(huh!) L-I-C
L-I-B-R-A-R-Y

L-I-B-R-A-R-Y
L-I-B-R-A-R-Y
L-I-B-R-A-R-Y
    That's how you spell it,
    Now what you gonna tell it?
It's been in your town for a hundred years,

So let's give the library three big cheers:
  Hip–hip–hooray!
  Hip–hip–hooray!
  Hip–hip–hooray!
When I say Library you say Card,
  Library (Card)
  Library (Card)
I got one today and it wasn't too hard.
  Library (Card)
  Library (Card)
Big brick buiding how sweet it looks,
Takes me on into the land of books.
P–U–B–(-)L–I–C L–I–B–R–A–R–Y
P–U–B–(-)L–I–C L–I–B–R–A–R–Y
P–U–B–(-)L–I–C L–I–B–R–A–R–Y

Book Lice

by Paul Fleischman

I was born in a
fine old edition of Schiller

          While I started life
          in a private eye thriller

We're book lice   We're book lice
who dwell   who dwell
in these dusty bookshelves   in these dusty bookshelves
Later I lodged in
Scott's works—volume 50

          While I passed my youth
          in an Agatha Christie.

We're book lice   We're book lice
attached   attached
despite contrasting pasts.   despite contrasting pasts.
One day, while in search of
a new place to eat

          He fell down seven shelves,
          where we happened to meet

We're book lice   We're book lice
who chew   who chew
on the bookbinding glue.   on the bookbinding glue.
We honeymooned in an
old guidebook on Greece.

          I missed Conan Doyle,
          he pined for his Keats

We're book lice   We're book lice
fine mates   fine mates
despite different tastes.   despite different tastes.
So we set up our home
inside Roget's Thesaurus

We're book lice
adoring
despite her loud snoring.
And there we've resided,
and there we'll remain,

We're book-loving
book lice

which I'm certain I read
in a book some months back
that opposites
often are known
to attract.

Not far from my mysteries,
close to his Horace
We're book lice
adoring
despite his loud snoring.

He nearby his Shakespeare,
I near my Spillane
We're book-loving
book lice
plain proof of the fact

that opposites
often are known
to attract.

Sam at the Library

by Carol Combs Hole

My librarian
Said to me,
"This is the best book for grade three."
That was the year I was in third,
So I took the book
On her good word.
I hurried home, crawled into bed,
Pulled up the covers over my head,
And turned my flashlight on
And read.

But the book was awful
And icky and bad.
It wasn't funny;
It wasn't sad.
It wasn't scary or terribly tragic,
And it didn't have even an ounce of magic!
No prince,
No dragon,
No talking cat;
Not even a witch in a pointy hat.
Well!
What can you do with a book like that?

My librarian
Tried once more:
"This is the best book for grade four."
That was the year I was in fourth,
So I took her word
For what it was worth;

And I took the book back home to bed,
Draped the covers over my head
Turned my flashlight on,
And read.

But the book was dull as a Brussel sprout.
I couldn't care how the story came out.
It didn't have baseball
Or football or tennis,
It didn't have danger and luking menace,
Or wicked kings like the ones in history,
And it didn't have even an ounce of mystery!
No midnight moan,
No deserted shack,
No great detective hot on the track,
Nobody tortured on the rack.
So naturally
I took it back.

My librarian
Used her head.
When I was in grade five, she said,
Sam, it's silly to pretend
You like the books I recommend,
When it's perfectly,
Patently,
Plain to see—
Your taste and mine will never agree.
You like sports books—
I can't stand them.
I don't like mysteries—
You demand them.
You think fairy tales are for babies.
You hate dog stories worse than rabies.

You're not me,
And I'm not you.
We're as different as pickles and stew.
So from now on, Sam,
You go to the shelf,
And pick out the books you want,
Yourself."

And ever since then
We get along fine.
She reads her books;
I read mine.
And if we choose to converse together,
We smile—
And talk about the weather.

Reading Is Dangerous

by Tony Johnston

Father says I'll break my neck
Mother says her prayers,
when I read my favorite book
going
   down
     the
       stairs.

SOME TRUTHS AND OBSERVATIONS
These might inspire thoughts to write about.

POEMS IN SOME TRUTHS AND OBSERVATIONS:

How To Tell the Top of A Hill • John Ciardi

Feathers • Joseph Bruchac

True • Lilian Moore

To Catch A Fish • Eloise Greenfield

Order • Myra Cohn Livingston

Courage • Emily Hearn

Cow's Complaint • Grace Nichols

Why Does Popcorn Pop? • Amy Goldman Koss

How to Tell the Top of the Hill

by John Ciardi

The top of the hill
Is not until
The bottom is below.
And you have to stop
When you reach the top
For there's no more UP to go.

To make it plain
Let me explain:
The one *most* reason why
You have to stop
When you reach the top—is:
The next step up is sky.

Feathers

by Joseph Bruchac

Everything that lives
wants to fly,
a Mohawk friend
said to me
one winter afternoon
as we watched
grosbeaks take seeds,
fluttering close
to our eyes.

Those were
dinosaurs once,
he said,
but they
made a bargain.
They gave up
that power
in return for
the Sky.

True

by Lilian Moore

When
the green eyes
of a cat
look deep into
you

you know
that
whatever it is
they are saying
is
true.

To Catch a Fish

by Elosie Greenfield

It takes more than a wish
to catch a fish
you take a hook
you add the bait
you concentrate
and then you wait
you wait you wait
but not a bite
the fish don't have
an appetite
so tell them what
good bait you've got
and how your bait
can hit the spot
this works a whole
lot better than
a wish
if you really
want to catch
a fish

Order

by Myra Cohn Livingston

You mean, if I keep my room clean
and never stuff things under the bed
and get straight A's
and be polite
and work hard
and never get in trouble
I could someday grow up to be President?
Forget it.

Courage

by Emily Hearn

Courage is when you're
allergic to cats and

your new friend says can
you come to her house to
play after school and

stay to dinner then
maybe go skating and
sleep overnight? And,

she adds, you can pet
her small kittens! Oh,
how you ache to. It

takes courage to
say "no" to all that.

Cow's Complaint

by Grace Nichols

Somebody calls somebody
a lazy cow
now in my cow's life
I ask you how?

If it wasn't so unfair
I would have to laugh
Dear children, as it is
I can only ask

Who gives you the milk
for your cornflakes
(crispy crunchy yes)
but it's my nice cold milk

that really brings them awake
children make no mistake

Who gets up at the crack of dawn
and works until the set of sun
Who eats up the grass
helping to mow the place for free
tell me if it isn't me

Who gives you hamburgers
Who gives you steaks
it's my meat they take
it's my meat they take

So the next time
you call anyone a lazy cow
think again, my friend, you'd better
especially if your shoes are made of leather

Why Does Popcorn Pop?

by Amy Goldman Koss

Popcorn does the strangest thing
   Of all the foods we eat.
Why does it pop and get so big
   When it's put over heat?

Popcorn kernels have a shell
   That keeps the moisture in
The kernel's shell is fairly tough,
    But also very thin.

When you heat the kernels up,
   The moisture turns to steam
If you make them hotter still,
   The pressure gets extreme.

The steam inside the shell expands,
    The kernel overloads,
   Till it's as full as it can be
  And "Pop!" the corn explodes!

14

 Mother Goose Rhymes

For a balanced introduction to the world of children's poetry, children should have access to the poetry of early childhood. Due to today's busy family work schedules and the necessity of babies and toddlers often spending a large part of their time with caregivers who may be from other cultures, many little ones just never hear the traditional rhymes. So, sprinkle your poetry breaks with an occassional Mother Goose rhyme or use several in a mini-program. We naturally think of using these rhymes with babies, toddlers or preschoolers, and primary-grade children, but the older children will enjoy them as a flashback to their own past. And, as they are so familiar to many children, they may be the perfect choice to help children who are presenting poetry for the first time feel confident.

You may already know the words to your personal favorites, particularly if you have a young child at home. For some reason, as soon as we become parents we seem to have total recall of the rhymes that we heard as youngsters.

When my daughter Hilary was born, I immediately began to recite these rhymes to her. However, I was disconcerted to discover that they made no sense in the real world. At a luncheon attended by respected early childhood experts, I told them that the Mother Goose rhymes were senseless. I was jumped on by everyone at the luncheon for my ignorance, insensitvity, and un-American thoughts. Properly chastened, I returned home and read and recited the rhymes to my daughter. She loved them, and I saw that I had been "playing professor" when I first read them, asking questions like: "What is the deeper meaning of Jack be Nimble?" "Why is Jumping Joan jumping?" Children naturally listen for and love the lyrical rhythm and the fun of the nonsense. They do not care at all what the historical origins are or whether there is a philosophical meaning to the rhymes.

Take the word of a mother and the experience of a too-intense academic: these rhymes are memorable, bouncy, and happy.

MOTHER GOOSE RHYMES

Little Bo-Peep

Old King Cole

Mary, Mary, Quite Contrary

Jack Sprat

Ride a Cock Horse

Three Men in a Tub

Jack and Jill

Jack Be Nimble

Sing a Song of Sixpence

Mary Had a Little Lamb

Hey Diddle Diddle

Little Miss Muffet

It's Raining, It's Pouring

Incey Wincey Spider

Jumping Joan

Yankee Doodle

The Poetry Break

Bow-wow

Higglety, Pigglety, Pop!

If All the Seas

Row the Boat

Humpty Dumpty

Twinkle, Twinkle, Little Star

Hickory, Dickory, Dock

Baa, Baa, Black Sheep

Little Bo-Peep

Little Bo-Peep has lost her sheep,
And can't tell where to find them;
Leave them alone, and they'll come home
And bring their tails behind them.

Old King Cole

Old King Cole
Was a merry old soul,
And a merry old soul was he;
He called for his pipe,
And he called for his bowl,
And he called for his fiddlers three.

Every fiddler, he had a fiddle,
And a very fine fiddle had he;
Twee tweedle dee, tweedle dee, went the fiddlers.
Oh, there's none so rare
As can compare
With King Cole and his fiddlers three!

Mary, Mary, Quite Contrary

Mary, Mary, quite contrary,
How does your garden grow?
With silver bells and cockle-shells,
And pretty maids all in a row.

Jack Sprat

Jack Sprat could eat no fat,
His wife could eat no lean,
And so betwixt them both, you see,
They licked the platter clean.

Ride a Cock-Horse

Ride a cock-horse to Banbury Cross,
To see a fine lady upon a white horse;
Rings on her fingers and bells on her toes,
She shall have music wherever she goes.

Three Men in a Tub

Rub-a-dub-dub,
Three men in a tub;
And who do you think they be?
The butcher, the baker,
The candlestick maker;
Turn 'em out, knaves all three!

Jack and Jill

Jack and Jill went up the hill
To fetch a pail of water;
Jack fell down and broke his crown,
And Jill came tumbling after.

Then up Jack got and home did trot
As fast as he could caper;
And went to bed to mend his head
With vinegar and brown paper.

Jack Be Nimble

Jack be nimble, Jack be quick,
Jack jump over the candlestick.

269

Sing a Song of Sixpence

Sing a song of sixpence,
A pocket full of rye,
Four and twenty blackbirds
Baked in a pie.

When the pie was opened,
The birds began to sing;
Was not that a dainty dish
To set before the king?

The king was in his countinghouse,
Counting out his money;
The queen was in the parlor,
Eating bread and honey.

The maid was in the garden,
Hanging out the clothes,
When down flew a blackbird
And pecked off her nose.
But there came a Jenny Wren
and popped it on again.

Mary Had a Little Lamb

Mary had a little lamb,
Its fleece was white as snow;
And everywhere that Mary went
The lamb was sure to go.

It followed her to school one day,
Which was against the rule;
It made the children laugh and play
To see a lamb at school.

Hey Diddle Diddle

Hey diddle diddle,
The cat and the fiddle,
The cow jumped over the moon.

The little dog laughed
To see such sport,
And the dish ran away with the spoon.

Little Miss Muffet

Little Miss Muffet
Sat on a tuffet,
Eating her curds and whey;
There came a big spider,
Who sat down beside her,
And frightened Miss Muffet away.

It's Raining, It's Pouring

It's raining, it's pouring,
The old man is snoring.
He got into bed
And bumped his head
And couldn't get up in the morning.

Incey Wincey Spider

Incey wincey spider
Climbed the waterspout,
Down came the rain
And washed poor Incey out.
Out came the sun
And dried up all the rain,
So Incey wincey spider
Climbed the spout again.

Jumping Joan

Here am I,
Little Jumping Joan;
When nobody's with me
I'm all alone.

Yankee Doodle

Yankee Doodle came to town,
Riding on a pony.
He stuck a feather in his cap
And called it macaroni.

Bow-wow

Bow-wow, says the dog,
Mew, mew, says the cat,
Grunt, grunt, goes the hog,
And squeak, goes the rat;
Tu-whu, says the owl,
Caw, caw, says the crow,
Quack, quack, says the duck,
And what cuckoos say you know.

Higglety, Pigglety, Pop!

Higglety, pigglety, pop!
The dog has eaten the mop;
 The pig's in a hurry,
 The cat's in a flurry,
Higglety, pigglety, pop!

273

If All the Seas

If all the seas were one sea,
What a *great* sea that would be!
If all the trees were one tree,
What a *great* tree that would be!
And if all the axes were one axe,
What a *great* axe that would be!
And if all the men were one man,
What a *great* man that would be!
And if the *great* man took the *great* axe,
And cut down the *great* tree,
And let it fall into the *great* sea,
What a splish-splash that would be!

Row the Boat

Row, row, row the boat
Gently down the stream,
Merrily, merrily, merrily, merrily,
Life is but a dream.

Humpty Dumpty

Humpty Dumpty sat on a wall,
Hympty Dumpty had a great fall.
All the king's horses and all the king's men,
Couldn't put Humpty together again.

Twinkle, Twinkle, Little Star

Twinkle, twinkle, little star,
How I wonder what you are!
Up above the world so high,
Like a diamond in the sky.

Hickory, Dickory, Dock

Hickory, dickory, dock,
The mouse ran up the clock.
    The clock struck one,
    The mouse ran down,
Hickory, dickory, dock.

Baa, Baa, Black Sheep

Baa, baa, black sheep,
    Have you any wool?
Yes sir, yes sir,
    Three bags full:
One for the master,
    And one for the dame,
And one for the little boy
    Who lives down the lane.

15

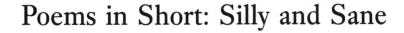

Poems in Short: Silly and Sane

Although the poetry break will rarely take more than a minute, there may be occasions when you will want to take even less time out of your very busy day. On the other hand, you may sometimes want to extend the poetry break with an extra treat by adding a short poem. These can be used at any time and can be repeated whenever you want a short time-out.

I'm not pushing memorization, because I think it's fine to read from a book. Children will see that you are reading and may want to pick the book up themselves and share or read a poem. However, these really are short enough to memorize.

The children will learn these quickly and may want to repeat them with you. In fact, these may be the rhymes you would like to have them present for another class, simply because they are so easy to learn, take no time to say, and also elicit a good chuckle or a satisfied smile.

Many of the selections in this section might be considered rhymes rather than poetry, but they are certainly lively. Perhaps they will inspire your audience to collect or write their own short pieces. Notice, too, that many of these are by that prolific and mysterious poet, the well-known Anon. or Anonymous. Since you will always want to give the name of the author of the piece you are presenting, this might be the perfect opportunity to explain the identity of Anon.—the designation that is given whenever the actual author is not known.

It is possible to string these ditties together to make their own theme program, or they can be put together as a subject theme. As an example, I've assembled seven animal poems to create a mini-program of short, silly animal verses.

If you use these mostly-silly poems in your poetry break, no doubt you will have a surprise visit from the district superindendent just as you are reciting about Dunderbeck's machine. She may well ask, "What are the educational benefits of this performance?" You answer, "I am showing the joys and wonders of humorous rhyme."

Enjoy.

POEMS IN SHORT: SILLY AND SANE

277

Mister Beers

by Hugh Lofting

This is Mister Beers;
And for forty-seven years
He's been digging in his garden like a miner
He isn't planting seeds
Nor scratching up the weeds,
He's trying to bore a tunnel down to China.

Rain

by Spike Milligan

There are holes in the sky
Where the rain gets in,
But they're ever so small
That's why rain is thin.

Come on In

Anonymous

Come on in,
The water's fine.
I'll give you
Till I count nine.
If you're not
In by then,
Guess I'll have to
Count to ten.

The Fabulous Wizard of Oz

Anonymous

The fabulous wizard of Oz
Retired from business becoz,
    What with up-to-date science,
    To most of his clients,
He wasn't the wiz that he woz.

Humpty Dumpty

Anonymous

Humpty Dumpty sat on a wall
Humpty Dumpty had a great fall.
All the king's horses and all the king's men
Had scrambled eggs for breakfast again.

Handyman

by Homer Phillips

No matter how tough the job
He never quits in despair
He'll stay right with it
Till it's fixed beyond repair

280

Dunderbeck

Anonymous

Oh, Dunderbeck, oh Dunderbeck,
How could you be so mean,
To ever have invented
The sausage meat machine?
Now long-tailed rats and pussy-cats
Will never more be seen,
They'll all be ground to sausage meat
In Dunderbeck's machine.

One day a little fat boy came
Walking in the store,
He bought a pound of sausages
And laid them on the floor.
Then he began to whistle,
He whistled up a tune,
The sausages, they jumped, they barked,
They danced around the room. Bang!

One day the thing got busted,
The darn thing wouldn't go,
And Dunderbeck he crawled inside
To see what made it so.
His wife came walking in just then
From shopping in the street,
She brushed against the starting rod
And Dunderbeck was meat! Bang!

The Young Lady of Lynn

Anonymous

There was a young lady of Lynn
Who was so excessively thin
    That when she essayed
    To drink lemonade
She slipped through the straw and fell in.

There was a young fellow called Hugh

by Max Fatchen

There was a young fellow called Hugh
Who went to a neighboring zoo.
    The lion opened wide
    And said, 'Come inside
And bring all the family, too.'

You've No Need to Light a Night Light

Anonymous

You've no need to light a night light
On a light night like tonight,
For a night light's light's a slight light,
And tonight's a night that's light.
When a night's light, like tonight's light,
It is really not quite right
To light night lights with their slight lights
On a light night like tonight.

Advice from Aunt Prudence

by Bobbi Katz

While sipping soda, NEVER guzzle.
While spooning noodles, NEVER slurp.
(Unless you're in Japan,
Where I understand you can!)

Numbers Game

Richard Armour

One runner's safe, one runner's out,
Or so the ump has beckoned.
The one who's safe touched second first,
The one who's out, first second.

The New Gnus

by John Foster

A gnu who was new to the zoo
Asked another gnu what he should do.
The other gnu said, shaking his head,
'If I knew, I'd tell you, I'm new too!'

Popalong Hopcorn!

by Judith Nicholls

I'm a hopalong
     popalong
popcorn in the pan!
         In
   out
      up
        down!
Catch me
    if
 you
       can!

Just Simply
Alive

by Issa

Just simply alive,
Both of us, I
   And the poppy.

MINI-THEME ON ANIMALS,
SHORT AND SILLY

Polar Bear

by Gail Kredenser

The secret of the polar bear
is that he wears long underwear.

Share:
Martin, Bill, Jr. *Polar Bear, Polar Bear, What Do You Hear?* Art by Eric Carle. Holt, 1991.
> Rhythmic text features the sounds animals make and hear.

Newton, Jill. *Polar Bear Scare*. Art by the author. Lothrop, 1991.
> Polar bears and other arctic animals chase a rabbit, but it's all a game of tag.

The Bear

by John Gardner

If somebody offers you a Bear, bow low
And say no.

Share:
Arnosky, Jim. *Every Autumn Comes the Bear*. Art by the author. Putnam, 1993.
> The large format and lovely art makes this perfect to share aloud. Watch a bear as he searches for his den.

Falk, Barbara Bustetter. *Grusha*. Art by author. Harper, 1993.
> Peter trains Grusha the bear to perform in the circus, but when winter comes Grusha grows restless for the forest.

Kinsey-Warnock, Natalie, and Helen Kinsey. *The Bear That Heard Crying*. Art by Ted Rand. Cobblehill, 1993.

285

When Sarah is lost in the woods, a bear protects her. Based on a true story.
Stirling, Ian. *Bears*. Photos by Aubrey Lang. Sierra Club, 1992.

A photo-essay introducing eight species of present-day bears.

Hippoportant Poem

by Mike Harding

A hippopotamus
Would squash a lot of us
If it sat on us.

Rabbit

Anonymous

A rabbit raced a turtle,
You know the turtle won;
And Mister Bunny came in late,
A little hot cross bun!

Share:
Watts, Barrie. *Rabbit*. Photos by the author. Dutton, 1992.

The color photographs of rabbits growing are worth sharing, although the text may
seem young for older children.

Good Chew

by N. M. Bodecker

People
chew Wrigley's
but
robins
chew wigglies.

Owl

Anonymous

A wise old owl sat in an oak,
The more he heard the less he spoke;
The less he spoke the more he heard.
Why aren't we all like that wise old bird?

Bird-noise

by Geoffrey Summerfield

Scrabblings
Squabblings
Scratchlings
Screechlings
Starlings.

16

Final Musings

Every surface in our home seems to attract books and papers. Once, we managed to keep the dining room table free of papers for weeks. We left a jigsaw puzzle on the table. Anyone who walked by was supposed to add a few pieces until the puzzle was finished. We were all disappointed when we discovered that the dog chasing the cat in a street scene in Paris was missing his head. We blamed the loss on our dog and went on with our daily lives. Russell Hoban uses the same sort of incident to muse about life in general.

It's impossible to know which poem will trigger a response in your listeners. Different people have different tastes and opinions about almost everything. These poems are grouped together because they are slightly more serious than some of the lighter, more amusing poems. Perhaps you or your volunteers will choose one of these to present when you or they feel the need to muse a bit about life. Poets can often best express what you are thinking or articulate what you haven't yet put into concrete images.

Poets are also able to take a small, passing thought and lend it layers of significance. When you hear or read a poem, you will often say to yourself, "I've thought of that too." Or maybe you haven't actually formulated a thought, but a fragment of a subject floats around in your head and you recognize it when it appears in a poem written by a poet who has had the same thought, but retained it long enough to shape it in words.

Any of these selections can be introduced with personal reflections, as suggested in the "Think about it" section and modeled with these poems, or can be introduced simply with the poem's title and author. Try to resist the temptation to elicit an oral or written response to these poems. Listeners may not feel comfortable articulating their emotions immediately after hearing the poem. Further, you may be disappointed to discover that a poem that touched you may not have moved everyone in your group. Be content to present a lovely poem with a significant message that may reach some of your listeners.

For greater impact, consider presenting the same poem more than once.

MUSINGS POEMS

Brachiosaurus • Mary Ann Hoberman

Kicking Up • Jane Yolen

Jigsaw Puzzle • Russell Hoban

I Hear the Usual Thump • Arnold Adoff

Unfair • Bobbi Katz

Neighbors • Yoshiko Uchida

Crush • Julie Fredericksen

from *Purpose for Radishes* • Martha Baird

Brachiosaurus

by Mary Ann Hoberman

This dinosaur is now extinct
While I am still extant.
I'd like to bring it back alive.
      (Unhappily I can't.)
The largest ones weighed fifty tons
And stood three stories high.
Their dinner ration? Vegetation.
      (Never hurt a fly.)
Alas! Alack! They're dead and gone
Through failure to adapt
And only known by track and bone.
      (I wish we'd overlapped.)

This poem contains intermittent asides by the narrator. Think about effective ways these comments might be presented—by another person, in another voice, or might you just turn your head to indicate that you are talking to yourself?

290

Kicking Up

by Jane Yolen

I don't know what bugs
My feet kick up
As I cross the meadow.
But frantic as a pup
A swallow follows
At my diligent heels
And eagerly accepts
My kicked-up meals.

This is the perfect example of taking a "small" thought and with just the right words making that small thought into a significant poem.

Jigsaw Puzzle

by Russell Hoban

My beautiful picture of pirates and treasure
Is spoiled, and almost I don't want to start
To put it together; I've lost all the pleasure
I used to find in it: There's one missing part.

I know there's one missing—they lost it, the others,
The last time they played with my puzzle—and maybe
There's more than one missing; along with the brothers
And sisters who borrow my toys there's the baby.

There's a hole in the ship or the sea that it sails on,
And I said to my father, "Well, what shall I do?
It isn't the same now that some of it's gone."
He said, "Put it together; the world's like that too."

More than one child will relate to the frustration of losing a puzzle piece through the carelessness of a sibling. In our house, we lose things because of our own sloppiness and the slyness of our pet ferret who hides pens, buttons and keys in a secret hiding place.

I Hear The Usual Thump

by Arnold Adoff

I Hear The Usual   Thump

And Know That One   More
                 R o b i n
Has Hit The Glass   Door
In Love   With   Its   Own
                Reflection

This Bird Seems To
            Be
R e s t i n g
     On The
     Ground
T e s t i n g   Its Bent
           Wing
I   Bring
A   Dish
Of Water And   Watch   For
            C a t s

We watched the robins build a nest outside our window. We watched as the eggs were laid and hatched. We watched as the baby birds were fed by their parents. And then . . . we watched as the babies were carried away by a hawk.

Unfair

by Bobbi Katz

It doesn't seem fair
that a tree
that makes such
a good place
to hang your swing
and gives shade
to people on hot days
and homes
to birds and chipmunks
could someday
get to be
a paper napkin.

Bobbi Katz might have written about toothpicks, paper party hats, or even spelling books. What else is unfair?

Share:

Edwards, Richard. *Ten Tall Oaktrees*. Art by Caroline Crossland. Morrow, 1993.

Ten trees disappear one by one as people settle the land.

Neighbors

by Yoshiko Uchida

Pigeon and sparrow,
Perched together
On that
Telephone line,

Do you ever
Talk to
Each other,
I wonder?

Or are you
Just strangers,
Like two people
Sitting
On a bus?

Does Andy, our pet ferret, wonder what we are thinking? Or where we are going? We are always imagining his thoughts.

Crush

by Julie Fredericksen

Philip, I wonder.
I wonder what your
favorite cereal is,
what kind of toothpaste you use,
what does your family do
on Christmas morning?
Do you open your presents
before you eat breakfast or after?
Do you have books in your room
and do you have cousins?
Does your dad get mad at you
and do you cry?
Do you go camping
and help put up the tent?
Philip, sitting in front of me,
your hair is sticking up today.
Why didn't your mother fix it?

Who do you wonder about?

from **Purpose for Radishes**

by Martha Baird

What is the silly radish doing
Making its root red
Underneath the ground?
The radish does not know that it is red;
It cannot see itself.
If there had been no one to pull a radish up,
No one would every know that it was red;
And radishes could go on for generations
Being red in vain.

This poem fits the category of musings perfectly. Others may think about radishes, but only a poet would decide to write about one.

Bibliography of Poetry Books

Now that you are totally addicted to the idea of presenting poetry to your family, students, relatives, friends, and coworkers, you will want to explore other sources for finding more poems.

There is an astonishing variety of poetry books at your library or bookseller, just waiting to be enjoyed. The lists that follow are meant to give but a sampling of the poetry books that have been published recently and the reliable standbys. You will want to add your own favorites, as you collect new volumes.

Adult Sources

Educators and poets have collected their thoughts on the uses and misuses of children's poetry. You may want to browse through one of these volumes to give you further insight into the subject of poetry.

Anderson, Douglas. *My Sister Looks Like a Pear: Awakening the Poetry in Young People.* Hart, 1974. Relates the author's experiences as a poet in a school program.

Arnstein, Flora. *Poetry and the Child.* Dover, 1962. Children as poets. An exploration of the relationship between teacher and child.

Booth, David, and Bill Moore. *Poems Please! Sharing Poetry with Children.* Pembroke, 1988. Two Canadian educators discuss how to bring children and poetry together.

Hopkins, Lee Bennett. *Pass the Poetry, Please!* Rev. ed. Harper, 1987. This practical, lively look at children's poetry includes ideas for introducing poetry to children.

Hughes, Ted. *Poetry Is.* Doubleday, 1970. A British poet shows how poets such as D. H. Lawrence, T. S. Eliot, and Theodore Roosevelt present nature and people through poetry.

Israel, Peter, and Peg Streep. *The Kids' World Almanac Rhyming Dictionary: A Guide for Young Poets and Songwriters*. Art by Heidi Sterson. World/Pharos Books, 1991. Organized by phonetic word-endings, this is intended for children—but useful for adults, as well.

Koch, Kenneth. *Wishes, Lies and Dreams: Teaching Children to Write Poetry*. Vintage, 1970. Discusses a method of teaching the writing of poetry. A companion volume is *Rose, Where Did You Get That Red?* (Vintage, 1973).

Larrick, Nancy. *Let's Do a Poem: Introducing Poetry to Chidren*. Delacorte, 1991. An overview of methods to introduce poetry to children.

Livingston, Myra Cohn. *Climb into the Bell Tower: Essays on Poetry*. Harper, 1990. An articulate exploration of poets and poetry for children. Livingston is both a poet and an anthologist.

————. *Poem-Making: Ways to Begin Writing Poetry*. Harper, 1991. A sophisticated look at methods for writing poetry, specificly designed for young people.

Padgett, Ron, ed. *The Teachers' and Writers' Handbook of Poetic Forms*. Teachers' and Writers' Collaborative, 1987. A dictionary of the different forms of poetry.

Anthologies

A collection of children's poetry is a useful tool for finding that perfect poem for your daily poetry presentation. It is interesting to compare the poems editors of various anothologies chose to include.

Booth, David. *Till All the Stars Have Fallen: A Collection of Poems for Children*. Art by Kady MacDonald Denton. Viking, 1989. Canadian poets are featured in this collection.

Cole, William. *Poem Stew*. Art by Karen Ann Weinhaus. Lippincott, 1981. Humorous poetry for children. Take a look at Cole's *Oh, Such Foolishness* (Harper, 1978), as well.

Daniel, Mark. *A Child's Treasury of Seaside Verse*. Dial, 1991. Poems and fine paintings go hand in hand in this collection.

dePaola, Tomie. *Tomie dePaola's Book of Poems*. Art by collector. Putnam, 1988. Holidays, seasons, animals, and people, all enhanced by dePaola's distinctive art.

Dunning, Stephen, Edward Lueders, and Hugh Smith. *Reflections on a Gift of Watermelon Pickle . . . and Other Modern Verse*. Photos. Lothrop, 1967. An exciting collection of contemporary poetry for young adults.

Elledge, Scott. *Wider than the Sky: Poems to Grow Up With*. Harper, 1990. Two hundred poems by a wonderful variety of poets. This collection is not illustrated.

Foster, John. *A First Poetry Book*. Art by Chris Orr, Martin White, and Joseph Wright. Oxford, 1979. The first in a series of several anthologies from Britain, this book is somewhat uneven in quality, but there are treasures here to find. The second book in this series is *Another First Poetry Book* (Oxford, 1988).

Harrison, Michael, and Christopher Stuart-Clark. *The Oxford Treasury of Children's Poems*. Illustrated. Oxford, 1988. Humorous and serious poetry for children of all ages.

Heylen, Jill, and Celia Jellett. *Someone Is Flying Balloons: Australian Poems for Children*. Art by Kerry Argent. Mad Hatter (c/o Slawson Communications, San Diego, CA 92103-4316), 1983. Traditional and contemporary poets are presented.

Hopkins, Lee Bennett. *Surprises*. Art by Megan Lloyd. Harper, 1984. A selection of poems especially for beginning readers.

Kennedy, X. J., and Dorothy M. Kennedy. *Talking Like the Rain: A First Book of Poems*. Art by Jane Dyer. Little, 1992. A substantial anthology compiled by two respected poets. Lovely.

————. *Knock at a Star: A Children's Introduction to Poetry*. Art by Karen Ann Weinhuas. Little, 1982. An introductory anthology with notes on form and feelings.

Larrick, Nancy. *On City Streets*. Photos by David Sagain. Evans, 1986. Just one of Larrick's many fine collections. This one features city poems.

Lobel, Arnold. *The Random House Book of Mother Goose: A Treasury of 306 Timeless Nursery Rhymes*. Random, 1986. You get both the 306 rhymes and Lobel's color art.

Prelutsky, Jack, sel. and ed. *For Laughing Out Loud: Poems to Tickle Your Funnybone*. Art by Marjorie Priceman. Knopf, 1991. An attractive collection of 132 humorous poems.

————. *The Random House Book of Poetry for Children*. Art by Arnold Lobel. Random, 1983. The favorite, with 572 poems, some poems in each section written by Prelutsky just for this collection, a subject index, and Arnold Lobel's art, too.

————. *Read Aloud Rhymes for the Very Young*. Art by Marc Brown. Knopf, 1986. Especially chosen for younger children, this outstanding anthology will be enjoyed by adults, too. Brown's art perfectly complements the selection.

Rosen, Michael. *The Kingfisher Book of Children's Poetry*. Illustrated. Kingfisher, 1985. Eve Merriam, Dorothy Aldis, and Mary Ann Hoberman are among the American poets represented in this British collection. There is a also a subject index in this volume.

Schwartz, Alvin. *And the Green Grass Grew All Around: Folk Poetry from Everyone*. Art by Sue Truesdell. Harper, 1992. Autograph rhymes, street rhymes, love and work poems— all together 250 selections collected by a noted folklorist.

Sullivan, Charles, ed. *Imaginary Gardens: American Poetry and Art for Young People*. Abrams, 1989. Poetry illustrated with American art.

Poetry for Younger Children

Although the poetry break encourages presenters to use all poems for all age groups, it is easier to have an audience listen down than up. These collections will be useful in quickly finding poems for toddlers and preschoolers that older children may enjoy hearing—or hearing again—occasionally.

Bennett, Jill. *A Cup of Sunshine: Poems and Pictures for Young Children*. Art by Graham Percy. Harcourt, 1991. Charming art and gentle poems for very young children.

Brooke, Leonard Leslie. *Johnny Crow's Garden*. Art by author. Warne, 1903. All the animals visit Johnny's garden in this nonsense rhyme.

Chute, Marchette. *Rhymes about Us*. Art by author. Dutton, 1974. Kittens, teddy bears, dinnertime, and other pleasures of childhood.

Cole, Johanna, and Stephanie Calmenson. *The Eentsy, Weentsy Spider: Fingerplays and Action Rhymes*. Art by Alan Tiegreen. Morrow, 1991. These fingerplays are illustrated with black-and-white cartoons.

Corbett, Pie. *The Playtime Treasury: A Collection of Playground Rhymes, Games, and Action Songs*. Art by Moira and Colin Maclean. Doubleday, 1989. Truly a treasury.

Cousins, Lucy. *The Little Dog Laughed and Other Nursery Rhymes*. Art by collector. Dutton, 1989. Familiar nursery rhymes illustrated with bold, primary colors.

Foreman, Michael. *Michael Foreman's Mother Goose*. Art by author. Harcourt, 1991. An extensive collection for Foreman fans.

Kuskin, Karla. *Soap Soup and Other Verses*. Art by author. Harper, 1992. In an I Can Read format, Kuskin offers short verses of childhood.

Lamont, Priscilla. *Ring-a-Round-a-Rosy: Nursery Rhymes, Action Rhymes and Lullabies*. Art by collector. Little, 1990. Expressive children romp through the is nursery collection.

Langley, Jonathan. *Rain, Rain, Go Away!* Art by collector. Dial, 1991. Lots and lots of sprightly drawings adorn the pages of this nursery-rhyme book.

Larrick, Nancy, ed. *The Merry-Go-Round Poetry Book*. Art by Karen Gundersheimer. Delacorte, 1989. Myra Cohen Livingston, John Ciardi, and Eve Merriam are among the poets represented in this endearing book for younger children.

Merriam, Eve. *Higgle Wiggle Happy Rhymes*. Art by Hans Wilhelm. Morrow, 1994. "How to Be Angry," "Keys," and "Banana, Banana" are a few of the poems in this delightful collection.

Most, Bernard. *Four and Twenty Dinosaurs*. Art by author. Harper, 1990. Nursery rhymes rewritten with a dinosaur theme.

Pomerantz, Charlotte. *Halfway to Your House*. Art by Gabrielle Vincent. Greenwillow, 1993.

Short verses about everyday life are illustrated with soft colors in an oversized format.

Prelutsky, Jack. *A. Nonny Mouse Writes Again!* Art by Marjorie Priceman. Knopf, 1993. Traditional rhymes and anonymous offerings collected in a picture book. Good source for short poems to fill out a program.

Poetry with Pictures to Share

These volumes are so attractive that it will be difficult to resist doing more than one poetry break a day. You might try reciting a poem in the morning, then sharing the poem with the art in the afternoon.

Baylor, Byrd. *The Best Town in the World.* Art by Ronald Himler. Scribner, 1983. " . . . that town where everything was perfect."

Bemelmans, Ludwig. *Madeline.* Art by author. Simon and Schuster, 1939. Rhymed text tells the story of a vivacious little girl.

Bruchac, Joseph, and Jonathan London. *Thirteen Moons on a Turtle's Back: A Native American Year of Moons.* Art by Thomas Locker. Philomel, 1992. Imposing full-color paintings help illuminate these Native American poems.

Carroll, Lewis. *Jabberwocky.* Art by Graeme Base. Abrams, 1989. A lush interpretation of the poem from *Through the Looking Glass* with double-spread paintings.

Charles, Robert H. *A Roundabout Turn.* Art by L. Leslie Brooke. Warne, 1930. A toad sets out to see if the world is really round.

Degan, Bruce. *Jamberry.* Art by author. Harper, 1983. With each line rhyming with the word 'berry', this is an exuberant nonsense poem accompanied by happy pictures.

de Regniers, Beatrice Schenk, et al. *Sing a Song of Popcorn: Every Child's Book of Poems.* Illustrated by nine artists. Scholastic, 1988. Nine Caldecott Medal winners take turns illustrating poems especially for children.

Farber, Norma. *How Does It Feel to Be Old?* Art by Trina Schart Hyman. Dutton, 1979. The advantages and disadvantages of old age are described in words and pictures.

Feelings, Tom, ed. *Soul Looks Back in Wonder.* Art by Tom Feelings. Dial, 1993. Poems by authors of African descent collected by the illustrator.

Florian, Douglas. *beast feast.* Art by the author. Harcourt, 1994. Short, pithy animal poetry and full-color art to share.

Frost, Robert. *Birches.* Art by Ed Young. Holt, 1988. Muted art leaves room young imaginations. Compare this with Susan Jeffers's artistic interpretation of the same poem (Dutton, 1978).

Giovanni, Nikki. *Knoxville, Tennessee.* Art by Larry Johnson. Scholastic, 1994. Double-spread paintings are perfect for this summer-day poem.

Greenfield, Eloise. *Daydreamers.* Art by Tom Feelings. Dial, 1981. Tom Feelings's portraits of black children are accompanied by a poetic text.

Grimes, Nikki. *Meet Danitra Brown.* Art by Floyd Cooper. Lothrop, 1994. Poems about being a friend and the color purple.

Highwater, Jamake. *Moonsong Lullaby.* Photos by Marcia Keegan. Lothrop, 1981. An original Native American lullaby with full-color photographs of people and scenery.

Koch, Kenneth, and Kate Farrell, eds. *Talking to the Sun: An Illustrated Anthology of Poems for Young People.* Holt, 1985. This anthology includes many traditional poems by American and British poets, accompanied by reproductions of fine art prints from the Metropolitan Museum of Art.

Lenski, Lois. *Sing a Song of People.* Art by Giles Laroche. Little, 1987. A celebration of city people.

Lewis, Richard. *In a Spring Garden.* Art by Ezra Jack Keats. Dial, 1989. Japanese haiku from morning to night.

The Little Dog Laughed and Other Nursery Rhymes. Art by Lucy Cousins. Dutton, 1990. Mother Goose offerings with big, bold, brightly colored art.

Livingston, Myra Cohen. *Light and Shadow.* Photographs by Barbara Rogasky. Holiday, 1992. Color photographs, large enough to share, enhance these nature poems.

———. *Space Songs.* Art by Leonard Everett Fisher. Holiday, 1988. Outer space is explored by a distinguished artist and poet. This winning combination has also teamed to give us *Sky Songs* (Holiday, 1984), *Earth Songs* (Holiday, 1986), and *Sea Songs* (Holiday, 1986).

Longfellow, Henry Wadsworth. *Paul Revere's Ride.* Art by Nancy Winslow Parker. Greenwillow, 1985. Parker's clearly defined art illuminates this famous story poem.

Manley, Molly. *Talkaty Talker.* Art by Janet Marshall. Boyds Mills, 1994. Bright, splashy art accompanies these bouncy limericks.

Pomerantz, Charlotte. *If I had a Paka: Poems in Eleven Languages.* Art by Nancy Tafuri. Greenwillow, 1982. Each of these poems uses a few foreign words.

Prelutsky, Jack. *Beneath a Blue Umbrella.* Art by Garth Williams. Greenwillow, 1990. Short poems and full-page art, this is a companion volume to *Ride a Purple Pelican* (Greenwillow, 1986), which features nonsense verse about place names.

Shaw, Nancy. *Sheep in a Jeep.* Art by Margot Apple. Houghton, 1986. Hilarious art matched to a funny, read-aloud verse.

Sing a Song of Sixpence. Art by Tracy Campbell Pearson. Dial, 1985. Delightfully illustrated, a pleasure to view.

Singer, Marilyn. *Turtle in July*. Art by Jerry Pinkney. Macmillan, 1989. Domestic and wild animal poems and full- page art for each poem.

Sullivan, Charles, ed. *Imaginary Gardens: American Poetry and Art for Young People*. Abrams, 1989. Contemporary and classic prints illustrate American poetry chosen for children.

Thompson, Pat, comp. *Rhymes around the Day*. Art by Jan Ormerod. Lothrop, 1983. Ormerod uses three preschoolers to illustrated this collection of nursery rhymes.

Westcott, Nadine Bernard. *Skip to My Lou*. Art by adapter. Little, 1989. The traditiona folk song gaily illustrated.

Whipple, Laura, ed. *Eric Carle's Animals Animals*. Art by Eric Carle. Philomel, 1989. Each of the animal poems is illustrated with Carle's double-spread art.

Willard, Nancy. *A Visit to William Blake's Inn: Poems for Innocent and Experienced Travelers*. Art by Alice and Martin Provensen. Harcourt, 1981. Visitors to the Inn range from the Cat of Cats to a wise cow.

Some Favorite Poets

Once you have found a poet whose work you particularly admire, you will want to search for more of his or her poetry. This list will give you at least one title by some of the most respected children's poets.

Ahlberg, Allan. *Please, Mrs. Butler*. Puffin, 1983. Best known as a picture-book author, Ahlberg writes about school and playtime.

Bodecker, N. M. *Water Pennies and Other Poems*. Art by Erik Blegvad. Macmillan, 1991. Slugs, moths, and other water subjects.

Cassedy, Sylvia. *Roomrimes*. Art by Michele Chessare. Crowell, 1987. Places, each beginning with a letter of the alphabet.

Chandra, Deborah. *Balloons and Other Poems*. Art by Leslie Bowman. Farrar, 1988. Thoughts about nature and self, illustrated with soft black-and-white pencil drawings.

Ciardi, John. *The Hopeful Trout and Other Limericks*. Art by Susan Meddaugh. Houghton, 1989. Humorous limericks by a popular children's poet.

cummings, e.e. *Hist Whist and Other Poems for Children*. Art by David Calsada. Liveright, 1983. This American poet is better known for his adult poetry, but these slections have been especially chosen for their appeal to children.

de la Mare, Walter. *Peacock Pie*. Art by Louise Brierley, rev. ed. Holt, 1989. Enduring poems from a master poet.

de Regniers, Beatrice Schenk. *The Way I Feel . . . Sometimes*. Art by Susan Meddaugh. Clarion, 1988. Children's ups and downs are offered in short, upbeat poems.

Edbensen, Barbara. *Who Shrank My Grandmother's House? Poems of Discovery*. art by Eric Beddows. Harper, 1992. Pencils, doors, and homework are among the subjects of these taut poems.

Edwards, Richard. *A Mouse in My Roof*. Art by Venice. Delacorte, 1988. An appealing upbeat collection worth presenting.

Fisher, Aileen. *Always Wondering: Some Favorite Poems of Aileen Fisher*. Art by Joan Sandin. Harper, 1991. A collection of some of the more popular of Fisher's work.

Giovanni, Nikki. *Vacation Time*. Art by Marisabina Russo. Morrow, 1980. From "Tommy's Mommy" to "Rainbows," these are poems with lilting rhythms.

Glenn, Mel. *Back to Class*. Photos by Michael J. Bernstein. Clarion, 1988. Outstanding poems illuminate the inner thoughts of high school students and teachers.

Greenfield, Eloise. *Honey, I Love and Other Poems*. Art by Diane and Leo Dillon. Crowell, 1978. Poems to make you feel and remember.

Hughes, Langston. *The Dream Keeper and Other Poems*. Art by Brian Pinkney. Knopf, 1994. The poems of an African-American poet first published in 1932, accompanied by appropriate scratch-board illustrations.

Janeczko, Paul B. *The Place My Words Are Looking for: What Poets Say about and through Their Work*. Bradbury, 1990. Contemporary poets discuss their poetry and give examples from their work.

Joseph, Lynn. *Coconut Kind of Day: Island Poems*. Art by Sandra Speidel. Lothrop, 1990. Rhythmic poems following a young girl's day in Trinidad.

Kuskin, Karla. *Near the Window Tree*. Harper, 1975 Notes precede each of these poems, which range in topic from bugs to friends.

Lear, Edward. *Of Pelicans and Pussycats: Poems and Limericks*. Art by Jill Newton. Dial, 1990. This would be a good book to introduce your audience to the master of nonsense.

Lee, Dennis. *Alligator Pie*. Art by Frank Newveld. Houghton, 1975. Lee is known for his nonsense rhyme.

————. *The Ice Cream Store*. Art by David McPhail. Harper, 1991. More nonsense verse from this Canadian poet.

Levy, Constance. *I'm Goint to Pet a Worm Today, and Other Poems*. Art by Ronald Himler. McElderry, 1991. Child-centered subjects from a first-time poet.

Lewis, J. Patrick. *Two-Legged, Four-Legged, No-Legged Rhymes*. Art by Pamela Paparone. Knopf, 1991. Astonishing animals in a collection by the author of the acclaimed *A Hippopotamusn't and Other Animal Poems* (Dial, 1990).

Little, Jean. *Hey, World, Here I Am!* Art by Sue Truesdell. Harper, 1989. Thoughts of school, family, and friends.

Livingston, Myra Cohn. *There Was a Place and Other Poems*. The thoughts and feelings of children with family problems, such as living with divorced parents, meeting fathers' girl friends, and dealing with lonely moms.

McCord, David. *One at a Time: His Collected Poems for the Very Young*. Art by Henry B. Kane. Little, 1986. McCord's work is the quintessence of children's poetry. A subject index is included.

McNaughton, Colin. *Who's Been Sleeping in My Porridge? A Book of Silly Poems and Pictures*. Ideals, 1990. This collection is uneven, but it includes some very funny poetry that children will love.

Merriam, Eve. *Chortles*. Art by Sheila Hamanaka. Morrow, 1989. Just one of Merriam's superb collections. Her trademark: a truly memorable use of language.

Milne, A. A. *When We Were Very Young*. Art by Ernest H. Shepard. Dutton, 1924, 1961, 1988. It is still a pleasure to introduce a child to Milne. Also delightful is *Now We Are Six* (Dutton, 1927, 1961, 1988).

Moore, Lillian. *Think of Shadows*. Art by Deborah Robinson. Atheneum, 1980. Shadows on the playground, in a tunnel, on Ground Hog Day.

Moss, Jeff. *The Butterfly Jar*. Art by Chris Demarest. Bantam, 1989. Funny, poignant, this gives Shel Sliverstein some competition.

Nash, Ogden. *Custard and Company*. Art by Quentin Blake. Little, 1980. From Nash, the suprme humorist, here are selections for children—and everyone else, too.

Pomerantz, Charlotte. *The Tamarind Puppy and Other Poems*. Art by Byron Barton. Greenwillow, 1980. Poems in English with a few Spanish words.

Prelutsky, Jack. *The New Kid on the Block*. Art by James Stevenson. Greenwillow, 1984. Prelutsky's poems are humorous, bouncy, and happy; they have great appeal for children.

Rylant, Cynthia. *Waiting to Waltz: A Childhood*. Art by Stephen Gammell. Bradbury, 1984. Portraits in poetry of a spelling bee, swearing, and people from the poet's childhood. More of this author's haunting poems from a youthful perspective are found in *Soda Jerk*, for which Peter Calanotto did the artwork (Orchard, 1990).

Seuss, Dr. (pseud. for Theodor Seuss Geisel) *And to Think That I Saw It on Mulberry Street*. Art by author. Vanguard, 1937. Marco's imagination turns an ordinary horse and wagon into a mammoth extravaganza.

Silverstein, Shel. *Where the Sidewalk Ends*. Art by author. Harper, 1974. The A-1 humorous collection.

Simmie, Lois. *Auntie's Knitting a Baby*. Art by Anne Simmie. Orchard, 1984. Lots of fun and some serious thoughts, too.

Sprika, Arnold. *Monkeys Write Terrible Letters and Other Poems*. Art by author. Boyds Mills, 1994. Nonsense animal poetry to amuse.

Stevenson, Robert Louis. *A Child's Garden of Verses*. Art by Michael Foreman. Delacorte, 1985. Numerous artists have illustrated this classic collection. This is a sophisticated interpretation of the well-known poems.

Viorst, Judith. *If I Were in Charge of the World and Other Worries*. Art by Lynne Cherry. Atheneum, 1981. The joys and worries of childhood. Some spoofs of fairy stories are also included.

Poetry for Young Adults

Give your young adults a treat with poems suitable to their tastes and interests. These books will help you select the perfect poem for middle grade or high school students. Also, search the library for adult poetry that may be particularly appealing to your young adult audiences.

Gordon, Ruth, ed. *Peeling the Onion: An Anthology of Poems*. Harper, 1993. Each of these poems prominently lists the author and date of writing.

Janeczko, Paul B., ed. *Looking for Your Name: A Collection of Contemporary Poems*. Orchard, 1993. The subjects of these contemporary poems range from thoughts on strip mining, suicide, and nuclear accidents to love, sports, and families.

————. *Stardust Otel*. Art by Dorothy Leech. Orchard, 1993 These poems feature Leary, the son of "flower-children" parents, who often hangs out at the Stardust Otel.

McCullough, Frances. *Love Is Like the Lion's Tooth: An Antholody of Love Poems*. Harper, 1984. A collection of poems expressing love by contemporary and traditional poets.

Poetry by Theme

It's convenient to find a poetry book featuring exactly the subject that you want to use today, but use these themed books to find new favorites and create programs you can use long beyond today or this week.

Adoff, Arnold. *All the Colors of the Race*. Art by John Steptoe. Lothrop, 1982. Thoughts and feelings of a child with a black mom and a white dad.

————. *Chocolate Dreams*. Art by Turi MacCombie. Lothrop, 1989. For chocolate lovers everywhere.

————. *Sports Pages*. Art by Steven Kuzma. Lippincott, 1986. Training, injuries, playing, winning and losing, individual and team sports are covered.

Bauer, Caroline Feller. *Windy Day: Stories and Poems*. Art by Dirk Zimmer. Harper, 1988. One of several anthologies of poems and stories on specific weather themes and seasonal holidays, including *Rainy Day* (Harper, 1986), *Snowy Day* (Harper, 1986), *Halloween* (Harper, 1989), *Valentine's Day* (Harper, 1993), and *Thanksgiving Day* (Harper 1994).

Baynes, Pauline. *Thanks Be to God: Paryers from Around the World*. Art by author. Macmillan, 1990. An interesting collection of multi-national prayers.

Bennett, Jill. *Spooky Poems*. Art by Mary Rees. Little, 1989. These are humorous poems featuring a Halloween theme.

Booth, David. *Voices of the Wind: Poems for All Seasons*. Art by Michele Lemieux. Morrow, 1990. An upbeat collection of seasonal poems.

Brenner, Barbara, ed. *The Earth I Painted Green: A Garden of Poems about Our Planet*. Art by S. D. Schindler. Scholastic, 1994. A collection of nature poems.

Brewton, Sara, John E. Brewton, and John Brewton Blackburn, eds. *Of Quarks, Quasars and Other Quirks: Quizzical Poems for the Supersonic Age*. Art by Quentin Blake. Crowell, 1977. The Brewtons have edited many collections. This one features poems about television, think tanks, and IBM.

Cassedy, Sylvia. *Zoomrimes: Poems about Things That Go*. Art by Michele Chessare. Harper, 1993. The ark, ice skates, and the subway are among the things that go in these poems.

Clark, Emma Chichester. *I Never Saw a Purple Cow and Other Nonsense Verse*. Art by collector. Little, 1991. Short nursery rhymes and nonsense verses in an attractive collection.

Cole, Joanna, and Stephanie Calmenson. *Miss Mary Mack and Other Children's Street Rhymes*. Art by Alan Tiegreen. Morrow, 1990. Rhymes for hand-clapping, ball-bouncing, counting- out.

Dahl, Roald. *Rhyme Stew*. Art by Quentin Blake. Viking, 1990. An irreverent look at some old folktales in rhyme.

Daniel, Mark. *A Child's Treasure of Seaside Verse*. Dial, 1991. Traditional British and some American poems featuring the sea.

Day, David. *Aska's Animals*. Art by Warabe Aska. Doubleday, 1991. Lush paintings accompany poems about wild animals.

Demi. *In the Eye of the Cat: Japanese Poetry for All Seasons*. Tr. by Tze-si Huang. Holt, 1992. Short, pithy expressions of nature.

Duncan, Beverly K. *Christmas in the Stable*. Art by collector. Harcourt, 1990. Christmas poems from the animals' point of view.

Esbensen, Barbara. *Who Shrank My Grandmother's House? Poems of Dicovery*. Art by Eric Beddows. Harper, 1992. Pencils, friends, and clouds are revealed in personal interpretations.

————. *Words and Wrinkled Knees: Animal Poems*. Art by John Stadler. Crowell, 1986. When the name or word for the animal becomes as important as the animal.

Fleischman, Paul. *Joyful Noises: Poems for Two Voices*. Art by Eric Beddows. Harper, 1988. Poems about insects, meant to be presented by two voices.

Foster, John. *Let's Celebrate: Festival Poems*. Oxford, 1989. Holiday poems from around the world.

Frazer, Kathleen. *Stilts, Somersaults, and Headstands: Game Poems Based on a Painting by Peter Breughel*. Atheneum, 1968. Poems related to the games shown in a sixteenth- century painting by the famed Flemish painter.

Goldstein, Bobbye S. *Bear in Mind: A Book of Bear Poems*. Art by William Pène duBois. Viking, 1989. The theme is bears, the art is by the bear expert.

Gordon, Ruth, ed. *Under All Silences: Shades of Love*. Harper, 1987. Kenneth Patchen, Paul Verlaine, Rainer Maria Rilke. Love poems for young adults.

Greenberg, David. *Slugs*. Art by Victoria Chess. Little, 1983. Not all adults will like this slightly gross, funny look at slugs, but children will love it.

Gunning, Monica. *Not a Copper Penny in Me House*. Art by Frané Lessac. Boyds Mills, 1993. Markets, hurricanes, and a Jamaican market bus are the subjects of these poems in lilting Caribbean cadences.

Hall, Nancy Abraham and Jill Syverson-Stork, eds. *Los pollitos dicen. The Baby Chicks Sing*. Art by Kay Chorao. Little, 1994. A collection of traditioal Spanish songs presented in both Spanish and English.

Hoberman, Mary Ann. *Fathers, Mothers, Sisters, Brothers: A Collection of Family Poems*. Art by Marilyn Hafner. Little, 1991. A picture book collection featuring family poems.

Hopkins, Lee Bennett, ed. *Extra Innings: Baseball Poems*. Art by Scott Medlock. Harcourt, 1993. Both pictures and poems are worth sharing in this baseball anthology.

————. *Ring Out, Wild Bells: Poems about Holidays and Seasons*. Art by Karen Baumann. Harcourt, 1992. Hopkins is a master collector of theme poetry. Other favorites *Dinosaurs* (Harcourt, 1987), *Good Books, Good Times!* (Harper, 1990) and *On the Farm* (Little, 1991).

Hubbell, Patricia. *A Grass Green Gallup*. Art by Ronald Himler. Atheneum, 1990. Ponies, horses, and horseshows.

Hudson, Wade, ed. *Pass It On: African-American Poetry for Children*. Art by Floyd Cooper. Scholastic, 1993. A picture-book collection of poems by African-Americans. Be sure to share the striking art, too.

Janecko, Paul B.,ed. *The Music of What Happens: Poems That Tell Stories*. Orchard, 1988. Story poems for young adults.

Jones, Tim. *Wild Critters*. Photos by Tom Walker. Epicenter Press (18821 64th Ave. NE,

Seattle, WA 98155), 1992. Excellent color photographs accompany each poem about Alaskan animals.

Kennedy, Dorothy M., ed. *I Thought I'd Take My Rat to School: Poems for September to June.* Art by Abby Carter. Little, 1993. Teachers, students, and math are among these school subjects.

Kennedy, X. J. *Brats.* Art by James Watts. Atheneum, 1986. One verse poems describing a variety of brats.

Knudson, R. R., and Mary Swenson. *American Sports Poems.* Orchard, 1988. Poems representing baseball, football, soccer, volleyball, and more sports.

Larrick, Nancy. *Cats Are Cats.* Art by Ed Young. Philomel, 1988. A lovely package of art and poetry—all about cats.

———. *Mice Are Nice.* Art by Ed Young. Philomel, 1990. Mice are the subject of this illustrated volume.

Lewis, J. Patrick. *July Is a Mad Mosquito.* Art by Melanie W. Hall. Atheneum, 1994. A poem for every month by a master of word play.

Lillegard, Dee. *Do Not Feed the Table.* Art by Keiko Narahashi. Doubleday, 1993. Short poems about household items: the coffee maker, toaster, and microwave oven.

Livingston, Myra Cohn, ed. *Poems for Brothers and Poems for Sisters.* Art by Jean Zallinger. Holiday, 1991. These are selected by a premier poet whose other collections feature mothers, fathers, and grandmothers.

———. *Roll Along: Poems on Wheels.* McElderry, 1993. Tractors, ice cream trucks, and trains are included in this collection.

Marzollo, Jean. *Pretend You're a Cat.* Art by Jerry Pinkney. Dial, 1990. Poems about pretending, accompanied by pictures showing various animals and children imitating them.

Mathis, Sharon Bell. *Red Dog, Blue Fly: Football Poems.* Viking, 1991. Touchdown, coach, and quarterback are some of the subjects covered in this picture-book-format collection.

McMillan, Bruce. *One Sun: A Book of Terse Verse.* Holiday, 1990. A great introduction to two-word poems illustrated with colorful photographs.

McNaughton, Colin. *Making Friends with Frankenstein.* Art by the author. Candlewick, 1994. A collection of silly, scary, sometimes disgusting poems about monsters that will delight children.

Merriam, Eve. *Halloween ABC.* Art by Lane Smith. Macmillan, 1987. Sophisticated Halloween poetry for older children and young adults.

O'Neill, Mary. *Hailstones and Halibut Bones.* Art by John Wallner. Doubleday, 1989. The classic poems about colors reissued with new color art.

Prelutsky, Jack. *The Dragons Are Singing Tonight.* Art by Peter Sis. Greenwillow, 1993. Double-spread art and poetry n a favorite subject: dragons.

————. *It's Halloween*. Art by Marilyn Hafner. Greenwillow, 1977. Prelutsky has written several holiday books, all published by Greenwillow, featuring easy-to-read poems, including *It's Christmas* (1981), *It's Thanksgiving* (1982), and *It's Valentine's Day* (1983).

Radley, Gail. *Rainy Day Rhymes*. Art by Ellen Kandoian. Houghton, 1992. The gentle art adds to the enjoyment of these rain poems.

Rogasky, Barbara. *Winter Poems*. Art by Trina Schart Hyman. Scholastic, 1994. A picture-book collection of poems about the winter season.

Sneve, Virginia Driving Hawk. *Dancing Teepees: Poems of American Youth*. Art by Stephen Gammell. Holiday, 1989. Short poems collected from the oral tradition of Native Americans.

Springer, Nancy. *Music of Their Hooves: Poems about Horses*. Art by Sandy Rabinowitz. Boyds Mill, 1994. Full-color art accompanies these horse-theme poems.

Steig, Jeanne. *Consider the Lemming*. Art by William Steig. Farrar, 1988. Excellent use of language and wit to describe a variety of animals, from the beaver to the penguin.

Streich, Corinne, ed. *Grandparents' Houses*. Art by Lillian Hoban. Greewillow, 1984. These poems pay tribute to grandmothers and grandfathers from around the world.

Strickland, Michael R. *Poems That Sing to You*. Art by Alan Leiner. Boyds Mill, 1993. Music is the theme, rock and roll and dance are among the subjects of these poems.

Turner, Ann. *Street Talk*. Art by Catherine Stock. Houghton, 1986. City poems about people, places (the museum), and street painting.

Wescott, Nadine Bernard, ed. *Never Take a Pig to Lunch*. Art by collector. Orchard, 1994. Sprightly collection of food poems.

Whipple, Laura. *Eric Carle's Dragons and Other Creatures That Never Were*. Art by Eric Carle. Philomel, 1991. Dragons illustrated with Carle's trademark colorful collages.

Yolen, Jane. *Best Witches: Poems for Halloween*. Art by Elise Primavera. Putnam, 1989. A prolific author gives us her views on Halloween.

General Index

Title Index

Title Index

Author Index

First Line Index

First Line Index

Subject Index